# Rest in the Day of Trouble

## The Life and Times of Habakkuk the Prophet

*by Kelley Varner*

D1559873

**Destiny Image Publishers**
**P.O. Box 310**
**Shippensburg, PA 17257**
"Speaking to the Purposes of God
for This Generation
and for the Generations to Come"
ISBN 1-56043-119-9
For Worldwide Distribution
Printed in the U.S.A.

Destiny Image books are available through these fine distributors outside the United States:

Christian Growth, Inc.
Jalan Kilang-Timor, Singapore 0315

Successful Christian Living
Capetown, Rep. of South Africa

Lifestream
Nottingham, England

Vision Resources
Ponsonby, Auckland, New Zealand

Rhema Ministries Trading
Randburg, South Africa

WA Buchanan Company
Geebung, Queensland, Australia

Salvation Book Centre
Petaling, Jaya, Malaysia

Word Alive
Niverville, Manitoba, Canada

# Acknowledgments

To all the local churches and individuals whose gifts made this project possible.

To Charlie Baird, elder at Praise Tabernacle and principal of Praise Tabernacle Christian School, who researched, edited, and wrote portions of Chapter Two.

To Pastor Rick Patterson, for his assistance in helping to compile the bibliography for Chapter Two.

To the Holy Spirit, who is my Teacher.

# Dedication

To all the members of Praise Tabernacle, Richlands, North Carolina, whose prayers, loving support, and ready response to the Word of God make it possible for me and my family to rest in the day of trouble.

# About the Cover

As Christian Americans, life flows by us in such constant turbulence that we need to hold on to the stability of Jesus. If we don't, we could be washed up along the shore and be lost. Like the waterfall, life today continually challenges our peace and safety. Thankfully, we have a solid rock on which we can build our "nests"; a rock that enables us to stand against and rise above any "trouble," and to "rest" in the peace of the Lord.

Cover Artist
Colleen Shea-Whitmire

# Table of Contents

## PART THREE: THE PRAYER
### Singing Faith

# Foreword

On the eve of his showdown with Goliath, David, the man after God's own heart, was given the armor of King Saul for protection. He had not proven it and refused to wear it. Proven things provide rest and security, leaving no surprises.

This book was written by a rested man who has made full proof of his ministry. He opens to his readers the rest and security of our Heavenly Father.

Mt. 11:27-29, NIV:

*All things have been committed to Me by My Father. No one knows the Son except the Father, and no one knows the Father except the Son and those to whom the Son chooses to reveal Him.*

*Come to Me, all you who are weary and burdened, and I will give you rest.*

*Take My yoke upon you and learn from Me, for I am gentle and humble in heart, and you will find rest for your souls.*

The rest that is *given* is our initial encounter with Jesus Christ. However, the rest that is *found* comes through a process: learning from Jesus. What we learn is the progressive revelation of the Father. Knowing and understanding the Father of love will produce rest in our lives.

Jn. 1:18, KJV:

> *No man hath seen God at any time; the only begotten Son, which is in the bosom of the Father, He hath declared Him.*

*Rest in the Day of Trouble*, written by my friend and ministerial colleague, Kelley Varner, is a declaration of Jesus, the Son of Man at rest in the bosom of the Father. The Prince and King of Peace is the pattern for the many-membered son, His glorious Church!

Is. 26:3, KJV:

> *Thou wilt keep him in perfect peace, whose mind is stayed on Thee: because he trusteth in Thee.*

Eph. 2:14, KJV:

> *For He is our peace...*

Jesus is our Peace. Set before us is a fresh vision of His Person and finished work. Through our God, we shall do valiantly. Together, we will "rest in the day of trouble!"

Pastor John Hancock
Agape Fellowship Church
Jackson, Mississippi

# Preface

I have been writing books for almost 25 years. This book is different.

Destiny Image and Don Nori have published four of my titles: the trilogy of *Prevail, The More Excellent Ministry, The Priesthood Is Changing,* and last year's release, *The Issues of Life.* Our own local church prints over 30 more books and booklets, including 16 volumes covering Genesis to Ezekiel. These Bible studies are addressed to Spirit-filled Christians, especially leaders.

*Rest in the Day of Trouble* is a word from the Lord to America. Even though its message is a warning, it is nevertheless filled with the promise of hope and comfort.

As the senior pastor of a local church, I am constantly dealing with people and their problems. I also travel throughout this nation, relating as a foundation ministry to many other assemblies. America and the Church in America are in trouble. There has never before been a day like this. We all need to experience the peace of God and rest in the day of trouble.

These are serious times for America. We now have a new president, a liberal congress, and a nation that has voted for its own judgment, choosing money over morals. The people of our nation are hurting. The Chaldeans are coming. Economic disaster, rampant immorality, and violence in our streets ravage the land. So it was in the land of Judah centuries ago. Yet out of that history comes the cry of a weary man of God. Like Habakkuk of old, we are all crying, "How long?" and "Why?"

This ancient prophet, born over 600 years before the days of Jesus of Nazareth, resorted to prayer and received a vision from the Lord. What did he see? How does it relate to us who must walk through the 1990s? Habakkuk's sob became a song. What was his secret?

This book will help you. Those who already know Jesus Christ as their personal Savior will be strengthened with might in the inner man. Those who have yet to give Him their heart will discover new hope and life. To each who reads this volume with sincerity, I bring good news. The answer you are desperately seeking for your family (especially your children), your business, your finances, your local church, your ministry, and your emotional well-being is set before you.

As I write, our armed forces are on alert. Will there be another war as we send our young men and women to police foreign "hot spots"? What about all the other travesties of justice, the atrocities that plague this planet? Is our own national debt about to swallow us all? How many hard-working Americans can really afford more and higher taxes to pay for health reform, a space program that seems to have failed, and other federal programs? Will the effectiveness and solidarity of our military prowess be destroyed over the gay issue? Are major urban centers about to erupt with renewed racial violence? Will the devastation of terrorist bombings happen more and more within our own borders?

What about your personal concerns? Is your job secure? Can your marriage withstand the economic and social pressures of the 90s? What does the future of this nation hold for your children and grandchildren?

This book is not only a contemporary commentary on one of the Minor Prophets; it is also an inspired message to rekindle hope in your heart. If you can see what Habakkuk saw almost three millennia ago, you will learn the secret of life. You will be able to rest in the day of trouble.

Pastor Kelley Varner
Praise Tabernacle
Richlands, North Carolina

## Chapter One

# The Day of Trouble, 600 B.C.

Ps. 46:1, KJV:

*God is our refuge and strength, a very present help
in trouble.*

The prophet Habakkuk lived in a day of trouble.
Desperately needing real answers, he cried out for help
to the Lord. Jehovah's reply brought comfort and strength
to His servant and the nation of Judah. That Word still
lives and breathes, imparting hope to America for the 90s
and the twenty-first century.

Before one can fully understand or appreciate this ancient writing, he must know something about the prophet himself, about the times in which he ministered, and
about the word that he proclaimed. So let us examine
Habakkuk: the man, the moment, the message.

### Habakkuk—The Man

The Book of Habakkuk is the Old Testament book of
*faith*. It was written by Habakkuk, the prophet of faith,

to the House of Judah about 600 years before the birth of Jesus Christ. Although often neglected, Habakkuk's prophecy is one of the most influential in Holy Writ. Habakkuk 2:4, the key verse, is quoted three times in the New Testament, more than almost any other Old Testament verse. It also is the only positive translation of the word "faith" in the Old Testament. It served as the basis for the Protestant Reformation and, through Luther's *Commentary on Galatians*, the conversion of John Wesley.

Hab. 2:4, KJV:

> *Behold, his soul which is lifted up is not upright in him: but the just shall live by his faith.*

Rom. 1:17, KJV:

> *For therein is the righteousness of God revealed from faith to faith: as it is written, The just shall live by faith.*

Gal. 3:11, KJV:

> *But that no man is justified by the law in the sight of God, it is evident: for, The just shall live by faith.*

Heb. 10:38, KJV:

> *Now the just shall live by faith: but if any man draw back, My soul shall have no pleasure in him.*

Habakkuk's voice was raised up to provide a commentary of the events of the late seventh century B.C. As in the case of the prophet Zephaniah, we are not even told the name of his hometown, though presumably it was in the south. *Adam Clarke's Commentary* suggests that Habakkuk was from the tribe of Simeon, a native of Beth-zacar (but offers no substantiation). The suggestions that he was the son of the Shunammite woman (2 Kings 4:16) or the watchman of Isaiah (Is. 21:6) have little evidence in their favor, as does the apocryphal story of Bel and the Dragon, which contains a colorful (but fictional) legend of Habakkuk's miraculous mission to Babylon to assist Daniel in the lion's den. In that tale his lineage is traced through the priestly tribe of Levi.

Some scholars are persuaded from a study of the prophet's oracles that he indeed was a temple singer and liturgist whose compositions were intended for worship. He may have been a member of the temple choir, hence a Levite (1 Chron. 23:3-6). Since he speaks of "my instruments" (plural), he may have been one of the musical leaders or directors.

Hab. 3:19, KJV:

> ...To the chief singer on my stringed instruments.

Hab. 3:19, NIV:

> ...For the director of music. On my stringed instruments.

Interestingly, the Dead Sea Scrolls, discovered in 1947 just before the beginning of the Latter Rain outpouring, included a late sectarian commentary on the Book of Habakkuk and furnished an important stimulus to a fresh study of this prophecy. The prayer of chapter 3 is omitted altogether, and although this bit of evidence seems to fit the higher criticism of those who regard the prophetic psalm as a late and secondary addition to the original work, it by no means proves the case.

The name "Habakkuk" means "embrace." It's taken from the Hebrew *Chabaqquq*, #2265 in James Strong's *The Exhaustive Concordance of the Bible* (Peabody, MA: Hendrickson Publishers, n.d.).

Hab. 1:1 KJV:

> *The burden which Habakkuk the prophet did see.*

Hab. 3:1 KJV:

> *A prayer of Habakkuk the prophet upon Shigionoth.*

This word, taken from the root word *chabaq* (Strong's #2263), is translated "embrace" or "fold" in the King James Version of the Bible. It is so rendered in Genesis 29:13; 33:4; 48:10; Second Kings 4:16; Job 24:8; Proverbs 4:8; 5:20; Ecclesiastes 4:5; Song of Solomon 2:6; 8:3; Lamentations 4:5; and also:

Eccles. 3:5, KJV:

> *A time to cast away stones, and a time to gather stones together; a time to **embrace**, and a time to refrain from embracing.*

The name "Habakkuk" has also been translated as "embrace of love, strong embrace, wrestler; embracing, infolding (with the hands or arms); a favorite, lover, struggler."

The reformer Martin Luther said, "Habakkuk signifies an embrace, or one who embraces another. He embraces his people, and takes them to his arms; he comforts them and holds them up, as one who embraces a weeping child, to quiet it with the assurance that, if God wills, it shall soon be better."

It is certainly not unfitting for "Habakkuk" to mean "embrace" or "wrestler," for in this little book we see a man, in deadly earnest, wrestling with the mighty problem of theodicy—the divine justice—in a topsy-turvy world. Some have called him the questioning prophet or the perplexed prophet. Then, as now, things sometimes do not make sense. Our wisdom and strength is not enough to meet the demands of the day. Like Jacob of old, we must learn to cleave to the Lord (Gen. 32:24-32; Acts 11:23).

The message of Habakkuk is vital to America and the nations. The 90s are "a time to embrace." This is the season to worship, to take hold of God with all our hearts. Again, the Book of Habakkuk is the Old Testament book of faith. The secret of faith is the love of God. Faith operates and is energized by love. When we embrace God, we release faith (Gal. 5:6).

There is a vacuum within man, each of us having been created with an innate desire to love and to be loved. When we fail to worship God, we will ardently run after other things to fill this void. Unfortunately, worship cannot be defined by the parameters of the external. Like the woman of Samaria in the fourth chapter of John's Gospel, we go from husband to husband (our varied external pursuits), but are never satisfied. Only God can fill the void (Ps. 107:9).

The Book of Habakkuk reveals the prophet's struggle to "embrace" the ways of God. Habakkuk first asks "how long" and "why" God will allow violence to go unchecked in His nation and among His people. The answer is given that God is raising up the Babylonians to deal with this problem. This brings even greater perplexity, since the prophet cannot understand the righteousness of punishing the sinful nation of Judah by means of a more sinful nation. A sovereign God, however, has the incontestable prerogative of dealing with the wicked in His own time and way. After praying and receiving fresh vision, Habakkuk finally "embraces" the justice of God's ways by unreservedly "embracing" God Himself. From this revelation flows his prophetic psalm of faith and confidence in God.

Phil. 3:12, NIV:

> *Not that I have already obtained all this, or have already been made perfect, but I press on to take hold of that for which Christ Jesus took hold of me.*

Almost 2,000 years ago, the Word was made flesh and dwelled among us (Jn. 1:14-18). Jesus Christ came to this planet as the fleshly, tangible image of the invisible God (Col. 1:15). God so loved the world that He sent His only begotten Son, born of the virgin Mary. Through the miracle and mystery of His incarnation, the Lord from Heaven "apprehended" us. That word in Greek is *katalambano* (from *kata* – "down" and *lambano* – "seize") and reveals the love of God "embracing" humanity. Now He eagerly awaits a people or a nation who will "embrace" Him with the same intensity!

2 Chron. 7:14, KJV:

> *If My people, which are called by My name, shall humble themselves, and pray, and seek my face, and turn from their wicked ways; then will I hear from heaven, and will forgive their sin, and will heal their land.*

Jer. 29:13, KJV:

*And ye shall seek Me, and find Me, when ye shall search for Me with all your heart.*

### Habakkuk—The Moment

This background of Bible history is necessarily detailed in order that we can understand Habakkuk's day of trouble. His prophecy belongs to the Judean period just prior to 600 B.C. At that time, the Chaldeans (Babylonians) were sweeping westward but had not yet reached the capital city of Jerusalem.

Hab. 1:6, NIV:

*I am raising up the Babylonians, that ruthless and impetuous people, who sweep across the whole earth to seize dwelling places not their own.*

Hab. 3:16, NIV:

*I heard and my heart pounded, my lips quivered at the sound; decay crept into my bones, and my legs trembled. Yet I will wait patiently for the day of calamity to come on the nation invading us.*

It would be helpful here to review the chronology of Habakkuk's era:

| | |
|---|---|
| 639-608 B.C. | Josiah's reign. |
| 608 B.C. | Jehoahaz reigned three months. Taken to Egypt. |
| 608-597 B.C. | Jehoiakim's reign. |
| 607 B.C. | Babylonians destroyed Nineveh, capital city of Assyria. |

| 606 B.C. | Babylonians invaded Judah. Took captives. First deportation (Daniel and his friends). |
| 605 B.C. | Babylonians defeated Egypt at Carchemish. |
| 597 B.C. | Jehoiachin reigned three months. Taken to Babylon. Second deportation (Ezekiel). |
| 597-586 B.C. | Zedekiah's reign (last king of Judah). Blinded and bound, taken to Babylon. |
| 586 B.C. | Jerusalem was burned, the land left desolate. |

Nothing is known of the personal history of the prophet. Habakkuk's ministry covered a period of about 20 years (620-600 B.C.), during the reigns of Josiah, Jehoahaz, and especially Jehoiakim of Judah. Others have assigned his ministry to the latter days of Manasseh's reign, but the best and most common view places his prophecy during the reign of Jehoiakim. Habakkuk was a contemporary of the prophet Jeremiah just prior to the Babylonian invasion.

At that time the Chaldeans had appeared on the scene as a rising world power and the coming enemies of Judah. They had obtained the throne of Babylon under Nebopolassar (625-605 B.C.). After the fall of Nineveh in 607, they began to push their conquests westward under the leadership of Nebopolassar's son, Nebuchadnezzar (605-562 B.C.). It was under this fierce king that Judah was subjected to their power.

Habakkuk's graphic descriptions of the Chaldean military exploits (Hab. 1:6-11) may point to the date 605 B.C., when at the battle of Carchemish, Nebuchadnezzar's forces proved their might and prowess by routing the Egyptians.

Their ruthless savagery is pictured by the prophet as a fisherman with rod and net. The Babylonians sat beside a pond which had been stocked abundantly with human prey. Pulling up fish after fish and eating to their heart's content, the Chaldeans then dumped the surplus on the bank to die.

No wonder the prophet cried out! How long was this outrage, this waste of human life, to go on? What pollution this was, strewn upon the shores of the nations! Why was this senseless brutality not being stopped by God's righteous intervention? Were the peoples of the earth to be destroyed without mercy?

Hab. 1:14-17, NIV:

> You have made men like fish in the sea, like sea creatures that have no ruler.
>
> The wicked foe pulls all of them up with hooks, he catches them in his net, he gathers them up in his dragnet; and so he rejoices and is glad.
>
> Therefore he sacrifices to his net and burns incense to his dragnet, for by his net he lives in luxury and enjoys the choicest food.
>
> Is he to keep on emptying his net, destroying nations without mercy?

The prophet's complaints center in the age-old problem of theodicy, whereby the sovereignty and justice of God's claims upon history are challenged by the overriding presence of the world's evil. Theodicy is a system of natural theology aimed at seeking to vindicate divine justice in allowing evil to exist. Habakkuk laments the prevalence of violence and injustice and seeks an answer to the question of why the righteous suffer and the wicked seem to prevail. This subject also occupied Asaph in Psalm 73: the affliction of the righteous amid the prosperity of the wicked.

Habakkuk's times had been predicted. Years before, the prophet Isaiah had forewarned King Hezekiah that his treasures would be carried to Babylon, and his sons would become eunuchs in the palace there.

Is. 39:6-7, NIV:

> *The time will surely come when everything in your palace, and all that your fathers have stored up until this day, will be carried off to Babylon. Nothing will be left, says the Lord.*
>
> *And some of your descendants, your own flesh and blood who will be born to you, will be taken away, and they will become eunuchs in the palace of the king of Babylon.*

But in Isaiah's and Hezekiah's time, it was Assyria whom Judah feared. Later, King Josiah of Judah was slain in battle just prior to the fall of Nineveh (608 B.C.). When the Egyptians came up to join their allies against the capital city, Josiah, who was a vassal to Nineveh, went out to resist the Egyptians. He was killed at Megiddo.

2 Kings 23:28-30, NIV:

> *As for the other events of Josiah's reign, and all he did, are they not written in the book of the annals of the kings of Judah?*

> *While Josiah was king, Pharaoh Neco king of Egypt went up to the Euphrates River to help the king of Assyria. King Josiah marched out to meet him in battle, but Neco faced him and killed him at Megiddo.*
>
> *Josiah's servants brought his body in a chariot from Megiddo to Jerusalem and buried him in his own tomb. And the people of the land took Jehoahaz son of Josiah and anointed him and made him king in place of his father.*

1 Chron. 3:15, KJV:

> *And the sons of Josiah were, the firstborn Johanan, the second Jehoiakim, the third Zedekiah, the fourth Shallum.*

Josiah had four sons. Of the first, Johanan, we know nothing (perhaps he died). His other sons were Jehoiakim, called Eliakim; Zedekiah, called Mattaniah; and Shallum, called Jehoahaz.

After Josiah's death, Jehoiakim and Zedekiah were passed over, and the people put Jehoahaz on the throne. After three months, he was carried away captive to Egypt by Pharaoh Neco, who put Judah under tribute to Egypt.

The Pharaoh then appointed Eliakim, Josiah's other son, to be king of Judah and changed his name to Jehoiakim. He reigned for 11 years (608-597 B.C.), his administration marked by taxation and moral evil. He was followed by his son Jehoiachin, and three months later by his brother Zedekiah, Josiah's fourth son. This irregularity in the Davidic succession reflects the confused state of the kingdom after Josiah's death.

2 Kings 23:31-37, NIV:

*Jehoahaz was twenty-three years old when he be-came king, and he reigned in Jerusalem three months. His mother's name was Hamutal daughter of Jeremiah; she was from Libnah.*

*He did evil in the eyes of the Lord, just as his fathers had done.*

*Pharaoh Neco put him in chains at Riblah in the land of Hamath so that he might not reign in Jerusalem, and he imposed on Judah a levy of a hundred talents of silver and a talent of gold.*

*Pharaoh Neco made Eliakim son of Josiah king in place of his father Josiah and changed Eliakim's name to Jehoiakim. But he took Jehoahaz and carried him off to Egypt, and there he died.*

*Jehoiakim paid Pharaoh Neco the silver and gold he demanded. In order to do so, he taxed the land and ex-acted the silver and gold from the people of the land ac-cording to their assessments.*

*Jehoiakim was twenty-five years old when he became king, and he reigned in Jerusalem eleven years. His mother's name was Zebidah daughter of Pedaiah; she was from Rumah.*

*And he did evil in the eyes of the Lord, just as his fathers had done.*

For about four years from the time of Jehoiakim's ac-cession, the people of Judah were left unmolested, except by the prophets, whose voices could not be silenced from denunciation and entreaty. In the case of Uriah, who prophesied against Judah and Jerusalem, Jehoiakim did try to rid himself of this source of annoyance. Jeremiah details the account:

Jer. 26:20-23, NIV:

*(Now Uriah son of Shemaiah from Kiriath Jearim was another man who prophesied in the name of the Lord; he prophesied the same things against this city and this land as Jeremiah did.*

*When King Jehoiakim and all his officers and officials heard his words, the king sought to put him to death. But Uriah heard of it and fled in fear to Egypt.*

*King Jehoiakim, however, sent Elnathan son of Acbor to Egypt, along with some other men.*

*They brought Uriah out of Egypt and took him to King Jehoiakim, who had him struck down with a sword and his body thrown into the burial place of the common people.)*

It was during these dangerous and turbulent times that God raised up the literary prophet Habakkuk, who wrote sometime just prior to 600 B.C. This is confirmed by Second Kings 24, which narrates the reign of Jehoiakim during the time the Babylonians began to harass Judah.

Thus Habakkuk, a contemporary of Jeremiah, was commissioned to prophesy during these fateful days (compare Habakkuk 1:6; 1:8; and 2:18-19 with Jeremiah 5:15; 4:13; 5:6; 15:10-21; and 20:7-18). Dark storm clouds were massing over Jerusalem. Josiah, Judah's last good king, had been followed by Jehoahaz, then Jehoiakim, the wicked king who burned Jeremiah's "roll" (Jer. 36).

Habakkuk took up his pen to write during the last two or three decades of Judah's history, and it may have been to Habakkuk that God first revealed how near the end really was!

Habakkuk knew that the reign of King Jehoiakim of Judah was full of injustice and bloodshed. The wicked king lived luxuriously in a palace he had built for himself by forced labor. Everything was awry, and God was apparently totally disinterested in the situation. But listen to the words of Jeremiah to this ungodly leader who loved money over morals. It is a powerful message to every leader in America, whether federal, state, or municipal.

Jer. 22:3, NIV:

> *This is what the Lord says: Do what is just and right. Rescue from the hand of his oppressor the one who has been robbed. Do no wrong or violence to the alien, the fatherless or the widow, and do not shed innocent blood in this place.*

Jer. 22:13-19, NIV:

> *"Woe to him who builds his palace by unrighteousness, his upper rooms by injustice, making his countrymen work for nothing, not paying them for their labor.*
>
> *"He says, 'I will build myself a great palace with spacious upper rooms.' So he makes large windows in it, panels it with cedar and decorates it in red.*
>
> *"Does it make you a king to have more and more cedar? Did not your father have food and drink? He did what was right and just, so all went well with him.*

*"He defended the cause of the poor and needy, and so all went well. Is that not what it means to know Me?" declares the Lord.*

*"But your eyes and your heart are set only on dishonest gain, on shedding innocent blood and on oppression and extortion."*

*Therefore this is what the Lord says about Jehoiakim son of Josiah king of Judah: "They will not mourn for him: 'Alas, my brother! Alas, my sister!' They will not mourn for him: 'Alas, my master! Alas, his splendor!'*

*He will have the burial of a donkey—dragged away and thrown outside the gates of Jerusalem."*

Jer. 22:19, KJV:

*He shall be buried with the burial of an ass, drawn and cast forth beyond the gates of Jerusalem.*

Jer. 13:22-23, NIV:

*And if you ask yourself, "Why has this happened to me?"—it is because of your many sins that your skirts have been torn off and your body mistreated.*

*Can the Ethiopian change his skin or the leopard its spots? Neither can you do good who are accustomed to doing evil.*

The hand of the Lord moved to fulfill the words of His servant. Jehoiakim refused to defend the cause of the poor and needy. Mighty changes quickly took place. The great Assyrian empire began to disintegrate; in 607 B.C. Nineveh fell. At once, Nebuchadnezzar of Babylon marched against the Egyptians under Pharaoh Neco, and utterly defeated him in battle at Carchemish (605 B.C.), an ancient fortress guarding the passage of the Euphrates. On this battle, which decided the fate of western Asia, the prophet Jeremiah wrote an ode of triumph (Jer. 46:1-12).

Jehoiakim, the "puppet-king" of Egypt, now became the "puppet-king" of Babylon. Totally self-serving, he submitted at once to the new conqueror and became his vassal for three years. Nebuchadnezzar's projects against Egypt were suddenly interrupted, however, by the death of Nabopolassar his father. In order to avoid a disputed succession, the young prince hastened back to Babylon. He broke up his camp and entrusted the bulk of his forces and booty to some of his generals, together with his prisoners (among them Daniel and the three Hebrews).

After three years' subjection to Nebuchadnezzar, the young and foolish Judean monarch revolted. The Babylonian king was busily occupied with his interests at home at the time and did not go himself to quell the insurrection. This policy did not prove altogether effective, and four years later when the king of Tyre rebelled also, Nebuchadnezzar felt it necessary that he himself should go and deal with the rebels. In that same year, Jehoiakim, who had fallen into Nebuchadnezzar's hands, was executed, and received "the burial of an ass" (Jer. 22:19; 36:30). It appears that his remains were afterwards collected and interred in the sepulchre of Manasseh, but he was unwept, unhonored, and unsung.

Such were the times of Habakkuk. Political unrest was the order of the day. The economy, immorality, and violence went unchecked from within and without. The leaders of the land were not leaders at all, only slaves to those who put them into power. Didn't God see all this? Didn't He care? How can one respond to all this? The answer lies in the key verse of Habakkuk's prophecy.

Hab. 2:4, KJV:

*Behold, his soul which is lifted up is not upright in him: but the just shall live by his faith.*

These words constitute the theme of this Old Testament book and stand at the heart of its theology of expectancy, which was Habakkuk's chief contribution to prophetic faith. The fullness of the "vision" was yet to come. Over six centuries would come and go before the seer's words would begin to be fulfilled.

But in Habakkuk's day, the law was "slacked," literally "chilled." It had been rendered ineffective, paralyzed. It had come to be looked upon as being without force or authority. Because of unrighteous judges, true law and justice had been set at nought. Most forms of judgment were corrupted; hence, life and property were insecure. The wicked were hemming in the righteous. Miscarriage of justice was the order of the day. Ensnaring the God-fearing by fraud, the ungodly perverted all that was right and honest. Because Jehovah did not punish their sins immediately, men thought they could continue to sin with impunity. But righteous judgment was at the door (Eccles. 8:11).

As mentioned, some believe that Habakkuk prophesied earlier, during the closing years of the wicked king Manasseh. Nevertheless, it is noteworthy that the final judgments against Judah and Jerusalem by the Chaldeans were directly linked to Manasseh's ungodly administration. The sins of the fathers had carried over to the sons and the grandsons.

Their most horrible practice was the sacrifice of human beings, especially children, to the gods of the heathen. To further understand the condition of the sinful nation under Jehoiakim's reign, consider the historical record of his evil great-grandfather Manasseh, one of the most wicked kings in the Bible.

2 Kings 21:1-5, NIV:

> *Manasseh was twelve years old when he became king, and he reigned in Jerusalem fifty-five years. His mother's name was Hephzibah.*
>
> *He did evil in the eyes of the Lord, following the detestable practices of the nations the Lord had driven out before the Israelites.*
>
> *He rebuilt the high places his father Hezekiah had destroyed; he also erected altars to Baal and made an Asherah pole, as Ahab king of Israel had done. He bowed down to all the starry hosts and worshiped them.*
>
> *He built altars in the temple of the Lord, of which the Lord had said, "In Jerusalem I will put My Name."*
>
> *In both courts of the temple of the Lord, he built altars to all the starry hosts.*

2 Chron. 33:6, NIV:

> *He sacrificed his sons in the fire in the Valley of Ben Hinnom, practiced sorcery, divination and witchcraft, and consulted mediums and spiritists. He did much evil in the eyes of the Lord, provoking Him to anger.*

2 Kings 24:1-4, NIV:

*During Jehoiakim's reign, Nebuchadnezzar king of Babylon invaded the land, and Jehoiakim became his vassal for three years. But then he changed his mind and rebelled against Nebuchadnezzar.*

*The Lord sent Babylonian, Aramean, Moabite and Ammonite raiders against him. He sent them to destroy Judah, in accordance with the word of the Lord proclaimed by His servants the prophets.*

*Surely these things happened to Judah according to the Lord's command, in order to remove them from His presence because of the sins of Manasseh and all he had done,*

*including the shedding of innocent blood. For he had filled Jerusalem with innocent blood, and the Lord was not willing to forgive.*

Manasseh was filled with wickedness. Horoscopes, witchcraft, sorcery, and seances polluted his court. Nothing was sacred, not even human life. He offered human sacrifices to the heathen god Molech, "the abomination of the children of Ammon" (see 1 Kings 11:7; Leviticus 18:21; 20:3-5; 2 Kings 23:10; and Jeremiah 32:35). The name "Molech" means a "king or ruler." The cult of Molech involved sacrificing children by throwing them into a raging fire.

Another idol who demanded live human offerings was Chemosh, the national god of the Moabites. Like Molech, Chemosh was worshiped by burnt offerings of child sacrifice. The name "Chemosh" means to "subdue." It can also mean the "powerful one." (See Numbers 21:29;

Judges 11:24; First Kings 11:7; 11:33; Second Kings 23:13; and Jeremiah 48:7,13,46.)

The god Molech and the god Chemosh were nothing more than evil spirits. They are still worshiped in America and throughout the nations, only now we call them "abortion."

For this shedding of "innocent blood," the Lord was not willing to forgive Judah. For 20 years America has filled the fiery laps of Molech and Chemosh with an annual offering of a million and a half of its unborn citizens! Will God forgive America?

Our government gains revenue by taxing cattle farmers for their yet-to-be-born calves in the wombs of their mothers. The same fiscal machinery loses money by allowing tax exemptions for human dependents. Is mammon a hidden motive for killing the unborn? Is a veal cutlet more precious than a human soul?

Manasseh's and Habakkuk's society not only killed its babies; it was marked by blatant, militant homosexuality and lesbianism, and had been for years. From Solomon's day on, a myriad of pagan gods whose temple prostitutes were both male and female had invaded the land. The gay/lesbian issue does not set forth a new morality or an alternative life style. It is the same old abominable immorality.

Manasseh's sins had reached down to the days of Jehoiakim and Habakkuk. Herbert Lockyer, in his *All the Men of the Bible*, says that King Manasseh of Judah was a man of policy. By 600 B.C., Judah had reaped the folly of:

> 1. *His policy of idolatry—He hated the first two commandments of Sinai, and reversed the reforms of his father Hezekiah.*

2. *His policy of immorality—Idolatry and immorality go together; thus there came the worship of the Assyrian Venus (connected with Chemosh) and a flood of iniquity over the land of Judah.*

3. *His policy of persecution—Manasseh allowed nothing to stand in the way of license and open evil. Martyrdom became the cost of service.*

4. *His policy of destruction—As far as he could, Manasseh destroyed the Word of God. Every copy found was consigned to the flames. So complete was this destruction that when Josiah, Manasseh's grandson, came to the throne, a copy of the Word was "discovered" in the temple.*

It is important to note that Manasseh did repent and turn to the Lord. The occasion for his conversion was affliction. While emprisioned in Babylon he prayed, beseeching the Lord, humbling himself before the God of his fathers. Penniless and penitent, his cry for mercy came from a broken heart, and God graciously received this prodigal king (2 Chron. 33).

Two generations later, godly King Josiah, Manasseh's grandson, rediscovered the Scriptures in the House of the Lord. The Bible was Judah's, and is America's, only infallible standard for right and wrong. Without it, there was and is no moral measure.

Godly King Josiah brought his people back to their foundations. The nation of Judah once again slew the Passover lamb. Something powerful happened as revival swept the land!

2 Kings 23:7-10, NIV:

*He also tore down the quarters of the male shrine prostitutes, which were in the temple of the Lord and where women did weaving for Asherah.*

*Josiah brought all the priests from the towns of Judah and desecrated the high places, from Geba to Beersheba, where the priests had burned incense. He broke down the shrines at the gates—at the entrance to the Gate of Joshua, the city governor, which is on the left of the city gate.*

*Although the priests of the high places did not serve at the altar of the Lord in Jerusalem, they ate unleavened bread with their fellow priests.*

*He desecrated Topheth, which was in the Valley of Ben Hinnom, so no one could use it to sacrifice his son or daughter in the fire to Molech.*

But Habakkuk's generation had not seen a move of God like this. King Jehoiakim was filled with evil and was finally bound in fetters by Nebuchadnezzar. Yet the Bible says that he "rested with his fathers." He was either not taken to Babylon; taken to Babylon and died there; or taken to Babylon and returned to be buried in Judah.

2 Chron. 36:6, NIV:

*Nebuchadnezzar king of Babylon attacked him and bound him with bronze shackles to take him to Babylon.*

2 Kings 24:6, NIV:

*Jehoiakim rested with his fathers. And Jehoiachin his son succeeded him as king.*

The historian Josephus says that Nebuchadnezzar came and slew the king, "whom he commanded to be thrown before the walls, without any burial" (Ant. X. 6-4). Jehoiakim mutilated and burned God's Book, and his body in turn was "drawn" (torn) and burnt unburied in the scorching sun. When we come to the line of our Savior's ancestors, there is a blank where a name should have been. In Matthew 1:11, we read that it was Josias, not Jehoiakim, who begat Jechonias. Jehoiakim's name is gone—taken out of the book of generations.

Jer. 36:30, KJV:

*Therefore thus saith the Lord of Jehoiakim king of Judah; He shall have none to sit upon the throne of David: and his dead body shall be cast out in the day to the heat, and in the night to the frost.*

### Habakkuk—The Message

Habakkuk's message is unique. Unlike the other prophets, he does not address either his own countrymen or a foreign people: his speech is to God alone. He is concerned about solving a problem which vexed his own sensitivity: Jehovah's government of the nations. The first part of the prophecy (chapters 1 and 2) is a colloquy between the man of God and God Himself. The remainder (chapter 3) is an exquisitely beautiful ode describing a majestic theophany—a visible coming of God to the earth.

The focus of Habakkuk's problem and prophecy is Babylon. Of the enemies that afflicted the covenant people long ago, three were outstanding—the Edomites, the

Assyrians, and the Chaldeans, or Babylonians. It was given to three of the Hebrew prophets especially to pronounce the doom of these world powers. Obadiah sealed the fate of Edom. Nahum brought judgment upon Assyria. Habakkuk dug the grave of Babylon.

Habakkuk's prophecy sets forth the problem as to why a holy God would use the much more wicked nation of Babylon to punish the wicked nation of Judah. More than 50 years ago, men asked the same question when Adolf Hitler came against France and Great Britain. God is consistent with Himself in view of permitted evil. He is holy and righteous and must punish sin.

In all this, the just are to live by faith. God's ways are right. Our confidence must not be based on God's favors but on God Himself. Our rejoicing in the midst of adversity must rest upon a total acceptance of the ways of the Lord. As stated before, our sovereign God has the incontestable prerogative of dealing with the wicked in His own time and way.

Habakkuk's prophecy naturally divides itself into three parts: the burden, the vision, and the prayer.

Hab. 1:1, KJV:

> *The **burden** which Habakkuk the prophet did see.*

Hab. 2:2, KJV:

> *And the Lord answered me, and said, Write the **vision**, and make it plain upon tables, that he may run that readeth it.*

Hab. 3:1, KJV:

> *A **prayer** of Habakkuk the prophet upon Shigionoth.*

The book thus divides itself into:

1. *The **burden**—The Problem of Faith (chapter 1).*
2. *The **vision**—The Answer of Faith (chapter 2).*
3. *The **prayer**—The Assurance of Faith (chapter 3).*

These three sections can be expressed in other ways:

1. *Chapter 1—The **sob**—sobbing faith.*
2. *Chapter 2—The **sight**—seeing faith.*
3. *Chapter 3—The **song**—singing faith.*

1. *The Burden—Faith grappling with the problem.*
2. *The Vision—Faith grasping the solution.*
3. *The Prayer—Faith glorying in the assurance.*

1. *Chapter 1—Faith Tested:*
   a. *The prophet's request (1:1-4).*
   b. *The Lord's reply (1:5-11).*
   c. *The prophet's remonstration (1:12-17).*

2. *Chapter 2—Faith Taught:*
   a. *The waiting prophet (2:1).*
   b. *The willing Lord (2:2-5).*
   c. *The woeful nation (2:6-20).*

3. *Chapter 3—Faith Triumphant:*
   a. *The Person of God (3:1-5).*
   b. *The Power of God (3:6-12).*
   c. *The Purpose of God (3:13-19).*

The Book of Habakkuk was a message of judgment aimed at the greedy nobles and the shameless religious leaders who were steeped in idolatry and who oppressed the common people of Judah. At the same time, God's promises were conveyed to the faithful, who were apparently dismayed that God had not intervened to vindicate justice.

The book has an historical purpose in that it comforted the faithful in Judah with the justice of God's coming judgment on the evil Chaldeans. Its doctrinal purpose is to teach the holiness and justice of God and the necessity of faith for the righteous, to show that God is just and that the just live by faith in Him.

The Christological purpose of the Book of Habakkuk is to reveal Jesus Christ as the "Holy One" (1:12), the One who justifies the righteous by faith (2:4), and the One who will fill the earth "with the knowledge of the glory of the Lord, as the waters cover the sea" (2:14). Jesus Christ is here revealed as the Judge of Babylon (Rev. 17–18) and the Rewarder of those that diligently seek Him.

Heb. 11:6, KJV:

> But without faith it is impossible to please Him: for he that cometh to God must believe that He is, and that He is a rewarder of them that diligently seek Him.

Like Job, Habakkuk neither used his questions to shield himself from moral responsibility nor shunned God's claims upon his life. He was genuinely perplexed by the unpredictable nature of God's dealings with him. He actually raised his protests because he thought so much of God, and hungered and thirsted to see God's righteousness vindicated. God's revelation of Himself laid the ghost of the prophet's doubts to rest and gave birth to a finer faith.

This powerful prophecy begins with a *sob* and ends with a *song*! What did the prophet *see* that so impacted and changed his life? What was his vision about?

What is it that can cause men today to rise up, to transcend the circumstantial, appearance realm? What can lift us up, out of our despair and into the place of faith?

When there is no visible evidence of God anywhere around us, how is it that we can still rejoice and "rest in the day of trouble"?

God showed me these answers, and I will show them to you. My friends, the Chaldeans are not coming to our nation...they are here! Their names are economy, immorality, and violence.

Before we explore all three chapters and each verse of this relevant prophecy, we must see that our times match those of Judah and Jerusalem over 600 years before Jesus was born. The Book of Habakkuk is the Word of the Lord to America in the day of trouble, the 1990s.

## Chapter Two

# The Day of Trouble, the 1990s

Hab. 3:16, KJV:

*When I heard, my belly trembled; my lips quivered at the voice: rottenness entered into my bones, and I trembled in myself, that I might rest in the day of trouble....*

The background of Habakkuk's prophecy reveals a time of great turbulence in the history of the nation from whom earth's Messiah would come. The same kind of pressures are flooding America today. The day of trouble in 600 B.C. has an uncanny parallel to the day of trouble in the 1990s.

The "Chaldeans" invading America are the failing economy, immorality (and the consequence of AIDS), and violence. Many good writers have focused on the money issues. My purpose in this chapter is to target America's moral problems. The outbreak of angry violence in this country is the manifestation of our frustration of having to deal with economic and moral dilemmas.

America's current political and spiritual condition is like that of Judah's in Habakkuk's time. Volumes could be written on the present state of our nation so we will but briefly sample the contemporary scene. I have included a list of recommended reference material for concerned citizens at the end of this chapter. Periodically throughout this chapter, I will reference the listed publication from which the information I am using was gleaned.

There is hope for our nation. Over the next few years, grassroots involvement will be essential to derail the liberal legislative agenda. In our democracy, the ultimate power resides on Main Streets across America rather than in the smoke-filled rooms on Capitol Hill. Letters, phone calls, and personal visits with your senators and representatives resonate with great impact. But all our efforts must be saturated by prayer. Learn God's telephone number and stay on the line (Jer. 33:3).

Each of us, especially our children, are facing unheard-of pressures. We may not agree with our President's hasty and immature decisions, but we must pray for him (1 Tim. 2:1-2). God can speak to him. He is learning that the majority of Americans are folks just like you and me. There are a lot of church-going sinners, but there are also people all over this great nation who love the Lord.

### A Word of Balance

In Habakkuk's day, Judah had sinned. The Babylonians were worse still. Jew or Gentile, both nations had grieved the Lord. Everything that Jehovah eventually judged Babylon for (the five woes of Habakkuk 2:6-19) was already at work leavening the citizens of Jerusalem.

The beast nature of man has not changed. The unregenerated human heart is desperately wicked. The same sins that beset Judah and Babylon then, plague America and the nations today. As then, men are lovers of pleasure more than lovers of God. It's not just Washington that is corrupt…man is corrupt! Satan knows that, so he has devised a myriad of religions to accomodate man's rampant idolatry. Our adversary is a crafty veteran with centuries of practice. He is the "god of this world" (2 Cor. 4:4).

1 John 2:15-17, KJV:

> *Love not the world, neither the things that are in the world. If any man love the world, the love of the Father is not in him.*
>
> *For all that is in the world, the lust of the flesh, and the lust of the eyes, and the pride of life, is not of the Father, but is of the world.*
>
> *And the world passeth away, and the lust thereof: but he that doeth the will of God abideth for ever.*

A final thought before we begin: hardcore, legalistic, right-wing intolerance and bigotry is as rotten in its hateful attitude and motive as the abominations against which it cries. Folks of such persuasion have a bad religious spirit. Many genuine Christians in America, like Habakkuk in chapter 1 of his prophecy, are trying to solve our problems with the brain and not the heart. They have become snared and distracted, obsessed with ultra-conservative politics. Our purpose in this chapter is to inform you and provide a means whereby you may be kept informed, not to stir up your soul to add to the current confusion. While Jehoiakim of Judah and Clinton of America have a lot in common, we are not anti-Clinton or anti-Democrat; we are for the Lord.

Many Americans, especially those who are Christians, are upset with our new President and his track record to date; however, his administration's sins only mirror the rest of our society. All have sinned (Rom. 3:10,23), and man at his best state is altogether vanity (Ps. 39:5). This chapter may appear to be negative, for it reveals the sins of our nation and its leaders. Bill Clinton inherited an office of confusion. He is weak because we all are weak. In the day of trouble, we have come to the end of our wit: our wisdom, intelligence, and skill. We will never call upon the Lord for ourselves or our nation until we see our need of Him. Only God can save America.

Ps. 107:25-28, NIV:

*For He spoke and stirred up a tempest that lifted high the waves.*

*They mounted up to the heavens and went down to the depths; in their peril their courage melted away.*

*They reeled and staggered like drunken men; they were at their wits' end.*

*Then they cried out to the Lord in their trouble, and He brought them out of their distress.*

Prov. 14:34, KJV:

*Righteousness exalteth a nation: but sin is a reproach to any people.*

2 Chron. 7:14, NIV:

*If My people, who are called by My name, will humble themselves and pray and seek My face and turn from their wicked ways, then will I hear from heaven and will forgive their sin and will heal their land.*

## Separation of Church and State?

Most Americans have never read the two documents upon which this nation was established: the Constitution of the United States and the Declaration of Independence.

The founding fathers were devout men who could not have been more emphatic in their determination that our national polity rest on a scriptural foundation. Of the 55 delegates to the Constitutional Convention, 52 were orthodox Christians. Historians studying the ideas that shaped our republic have shown that scriptural citations dwarf all individual influences, as the Bible was quoted 34 percent of the time! By today's standards, the founding fathers were the religious right. It's time to return to our foundations (see reference no. 17).

The words "separation of church and state" are familiar to all of us. The average American believes that this phrase appears in our Constitution. It does not!

The phrase "separation of church and state" was first used by President Thomas Jefferson in a letter addressing a group of Baptists. He assured them that the government, or "state," would not establish one "denomination" as the state religion. The phrase "a wall of separatism" was uttered by a prominent Baptist minister named Roger Williams. He was referring to a wall of separation between the "garden of the Church" and the "wilderness of the world." His pure meaning and intent was to protect the church from government intrusion.

In 1947, the Supreme Court first declared the existence of a separation of church and state in the First Amendment.

Nothing could be further from the truth.

The Court accomplished this by improperly linking the Fourteenth Amendment (which assured former slaves of their right to citizenship in all the states) to the First Amendment, and then applying it against the states.

This was not only unprecedented...it was absurd. Christian principles had been taught in our public schools for over 340 years—170 of those years *under the Constitution.* The landmark decision of 1947 opened the door. Then in 1962, what America had been doing for decades was declared to be unconstitutional: the Supreme Court decided to prohibit prayer in public schools.

Our schools and our nation have never been the same. Since those historic decisions in 1947 and 1962, America has radically changed (see reference no. 21).

Furthermore, underlying the Declaration of Independence is a foundation of biblical principles and Christian influence. The Bible and Christianity, not deism and secularism, were the most important influences on the framers. Sadly, the American educational system denies or ignores almost all the evidence of this fact. Someone has said, "Where we take America in the future depends in part on where we think she came from."

The American Revolution is not over. The ideals enshrined in the Declaration for which the founders fought and died—ideals of law, justice, equality, liberty, inalienable rights, self-government—are barely understood in America today, much less in the rest of the world.

The American Revolution was more than a contest with England. It was and is a war of ideas, a contest for the hearts and minds of men which defended a vision about the God-given dignity of man. This vision was inspired over time by the words of the Bible and the teachings of Christianity, but applies to all men everywhere regardless of their faith.

Now, however, the Declaration's ideas are scoffed at by philosophers, misrepresented by historians, attacked by clergymen, ridiculed by law professors, held in contempt by power-hungry politicians, and ignored by the people. As long as this continues, the American Revolution is not over.

It is important, particularly for Christians, to know that the Declaration of Independence stands in the Judeo-Christian stream of political theory. Its legacy must be defended, since the War for Independence was different both in degree and in kind from its secular counterpart, the French Revolution. We must proclaim that legacy of political and spiritual liberty (see reference no. 9).

### Child Sacrifice

Hab. 2:10, NIV:

*You have plotted the ruin of many peoples, shaming your own house and forfeiting your life.*

America began as a Christian nation, the Bible its moral and ethical base. Godly character and solid moral values ranked high. The founding fathers would be shocked to know America's besetting sin: the murdering of its unborn, the crime of abortion!

The sin for which Jehovah could not forgive Judah and Jehoiakim was the killing of her children, making them pass through the fire to Chemosh and Molech, the gods of Moab and Ammon. The sin of America is abortion and child abuse. That is obvious. What is not-so-obvious is that we have ruined our children by offering them up to the gods of secular humanism.

Two days after taking office, our President suspended the so-called Title X "Gag Rule," lifted the ban on fetal tissue research, reversed the ban on abortions in military hospitals, paved the way for importation of the RU-486 abortion pill, and lifted restrictions on foreign aid which funds abortions (see reference no. 5).

Dr. Joycelyn Elders, Bill Clinton's choice for Surgeon General, plans to institute explicit, no holds barred, sex education beginning with kindergartners. She advises pro-lifers to "get over their love affair with the fetus." She wants to pour more money into a very expensive program that has proven in Arkansas to be an accelerator of both teenage pregnancy and abortions. While speaking at the Association of Reproductive Health Professionals Conference in January of 1993, she said, "We've taught our children in driver's education what to do in the front seat, and now we've got to teach them what to do in the back seat" (see reference no. 17).

Dr. Elders would love this: a Louisiana court has found "unconstitutional" a local sex-education curriculum that suggests abstinence as a *possible* means of avoiding unwanted pregnancies and sexual diseases (see reference no. 22).

When will Americans understand that "safe sex" is only possible when two virgins marry each other and are faithful for a lifetime?

Heb. 13:4, KJV:

*Marriage is honourable in all, and the bed undefiled: but whoremongers and adulterers God will judge.*

Heb. 13:4, NIV:

*Marriage should be honored by all, and the marriage bed kept pure, for God will judge the adulterer and all the sexually immoral.*

Part of the new administration's legislative agenda is to allow abortion on demand through nine months of pregnancy. FOCA, the Freedom of Choice Act (S. 25 and H.R. 25), the so-called "Kill Bill," is the butcher's instrument. At the time of this writing, FOCA was still in committee. The House version of this bill (as of May 1993) would:

1. *Overturn prohibitions on third trimester abortions.*
2. *Deny parents any involvement in their child's decision to abort.*
3. *Allow non-physicians to perform abortions.*
4. *Prohibit waiting periods.*
5. *Outlaw conscience statutes that protect religious hospitals from having to provide abortions.*

> 6. *Invalidate informed consent laws for abortion which serve to provide women with meaningful information regarding the development of children in the womb as well as alternatives to abortion.*

FOCA may even require states to use taxpayers' funds to pay for some abortions. In other words, FOCA would allow abortion on demand through the nine months of pregnancy in all 50 states and the territories. If this bill becomes law, your 13-year-old daughter will be able to get a risky late-term abortion from an unlicensed practitioner without your consent. May God help us (see reference no. 17).

President Clinton says that his pro-choice position was influenced in Bible study with his former pastor, the late W.O. Vaught. Clinton says that "[Vaught] read the meaning of life and birth and personhood in words which literally meant, 'to breathe life into,' so he thought the most literal meaning of life in the Bible would be to conclude that it began at birth" (see reference no. 5). Read it again, sir.

Gen. 25:23, NIV:

> *The Lord said to her, "Two nations are in your womb, and two peoples from within you will be separated; one people will be stronger than the other, and the older will serve the younger."*

Ps. 139:13, NIV:

> *For You created my inmost being; You knit me together in my mother's womb.*

Jer. 1:5, NIV:

*Before I formed you in the womb I knew you, before you were born I set you apart; I appointed you as a prophet to the nations.*

Lk. 1:15, KJV:

*For He shall be great in the sight of the Lord, and shall drink neither wine nor strong drink; and He shall be filled with the Holy Ghost, even from His mother's womb.*

Lk. 1:44, NIV:

*As soon as the sound of your greeting reached my ears, the baby in my womb leaped for joy.*

Lk. 2:21, KJV:

*And when eight days were accomplished for the circumcising of the child, His name was called JESUS, which was so named of the angel before He was conceived in the womb.*

The statistics are horrifying. According to the American Enterprise Institute, teenage sexual activity now results in nearly one million pregnancies annually, leading to 406,000 abortions, 134,000 miscarriages, and 490,000 live births. About three million teens will get a sexually transmitted disease this year. The President's new abortion rulings will assuredly add to the already staggering 1.6 million annual abortions. That's 4,380 every day (see reference no. 15).

Since the legalization of abortion in 1973 (*Roe vs. Wade*), there have been more than 28 million abortions in the United States. The statistics in 1990 showed that 24.6 percent of all pregnancies in this nation ended in abortion (see reference no. 16).

The United States has the most permissive abortion laws of any democracy. But "child sacrifice" in this nation does not stop with the outrage of killing babies in the womb; it continues with the crime of child abuse in the home.

The number of children abused in the United States has increased dramatically in the past two decades. There were 669,000 reported cases in 1976. This rose to 2,694,000 reported cases in 1990. Some of the reasons for the dramatic increase in child abuse in this nation are substance abuse, the additional stress of single parenthood, and poverty (see reference no. 16).

We must save the children. One of the most degenerating factors contributing to child neglect (hence spiritual retardation) and leading to spiritual death has been the dissolution of the nuclear family. This has been aggravated by our culture's moral decay and by an apathetic attitude toward scholastic and spiritual excellence. Listed below are some government-enhanced (one would hope unwittingly so) hindrances to the socially, economically, and spiritually balanced family (see reference no. 16).

1. *Restrictive choice of schools.*
2. *Loose and non-existent national standards for academic excellence.*
3. *Dogmatic certification that does not insure curricular or instructional excellence.*

4. *A welfare system that imposes economic penalties on single mothers who want to get married.*

5. *Economic barriers that limit the desirability of enterprise zones, and tenant ownership, thus maintaining the poverty of urbanites and the underclass.*

6. *Meager personal dependent exemptions ($2,300) that do little to support or encourage the family unit.*

7. *Lax, no-fault divorce laws for parents with children.*

8. *Tedious and obstructive procedures for adoption.*

9. *No centralized effort (for example, the IRS) to recover or collect child-support payments except through litigation.*

10. *No process in place to identify the father of every child by name and social security number.*

11. *No legal process to encourage fathers to legitimize their children, attend school, and find gainful employment.*

The lap of Molech is also the fiery lap of secular humanism. The new administration, especially the President's wife, has advocated massive and immediate expansion of federal child-care programs. But do you know the real philosophy of the First Lady from Little Rock? The image of Mrs. Clinton that has crystallized in the public consciousness is a woman with consuming ambition, inflexibility of purpose, domination of a pliable husband, and an unsettling lack of tender human feeling, along with the affluent feminist's contempt for traditional female roles.

President Clinton has abandoned the husband-and-wife team presidency concept implicit in the slogan, "Buy one, get one free"; yet Hillary stands well to the left of her husband and enjoys an independent power base within his coalition. No one in the press has really scrutinized her 20 years of political activism in the far left regions of the Democratic party. She graduated from Wellesley and went to Yale Law School where she met her future husband, and where law school professor Burke Marshall took her under her wing. Marshall, a Kennedy family confidante, is the first person Ted Kennedy called after driving Mary Jo Kopechne off Chappaquiddick Bridge. While at Yale, Hillary slipped into an intellectual milieu marked by way-out and sometimes vicious left-wing polemics and activism, including the leading of campus protests against the Vietnam War.

In her *Children Under the Law* (a 1974 essay reprinted by the Harvard Educational Review in 1982), Hillary called for a radical redefinition of the relationship between state and family. As a champion of the "children's rights" movement, she proposed three measures:

1. *The immediate abolition of the legal status of minority and the reversal of the legal presumption of the incompetence of minors in favor of a presumption of competence.*
2. *The extension to children of all procedural rights guaranteed to adults.*
3. *The rejection of the legal presumption of the identity of interests between parents and their children, and permission for competent children to assert those independent interests in the courts.*

In effect, when parents and their teenage kids don't agree on who's the boss, a judge steps in! Over one million North American families were falsely accused of child abuse in 1992. Children are being torn away from their families and thrown into state care. Parents have been stripped of their Constitutional rights. The Children's Defense Fund is the chief vehicle for those who want government to take over the raising of our children. Mrs. Clinton, a long-time supporter of the CDF, exemplifies the mentality of many of our nation's leaders who harbor a deeply cynical view of the traditional family and its origins. In *Children Under the Law*, she equates the family with slavery:

"The basic rationale for depriving people of rights in a dependency relationship is that certain individuals are incapable or undeserving of the right to take care of themselves, and consequently need social institutions specifically designed to safeguard their position. Along with the family, past and present examples of such arrangements include marriage, slavery, and the Indian reservation system" (see reference no. 2).

Lev. 18:21, KJV:

*And thou shalt not let any of thy seed pass through the fire to Molech, neither shalt thou profane the name of thy God: I am the Lord.*

Deut. 18:9-12, NIV:

*When you enter the land the Lord your God is giving you, do not learn to imitate the detestable ways of the nations there.*

*Let no one be found among you who sacrifices his son or daughter in the fire, who practices divination or sorcery, interprets omens, engages in witchcraft,*

*or casts spells, or who is a medium or spiritist or who consults the dead.*

*Anyone who does these things is detestable to the Lord, and because of these detestable practices the Lord your God will drive out those nations before you.*

Jer. 32:35, NIV:

*They built high places for Baal in the Valley of Ben Hinnom to sacrifice their sons and daughters to Molech, though I never commanded, nor did it enter My mind, that they should do such a detestable thing and so make Judah sin.*

2 Kings 24:3-4, NIV:

*Surely these things happened to Judah according to the Lord's command, in order to remove them from His presence because of the sins of Manasseh and all he had done,*

*including the shedding of innocent blood. For he had filled Jerusalem with innocent blood, and the Lord was not willing to forgive.*

## Religion and Politics

Hab. 1:11, NIV:

*Then they sweep past like the wind and go on—guilty men, whose own strength is their god.*

One's views on the abortion question and every other issue are shaped by one's religious beliefs. Just as there is a religious right, so there is a religious left. No longer sidelined, the religious left's domestic agenda is now shared by all branches of the Washington political establishment: abortion rights, homosexual rights, sex education and condom distribution in the public schools, tax-and-spend government economics, and federally funded health care (see reference no. 29).

In the presidential campaigns of 1980 and 1984, when some Republicans and conservative ministers brought religion and quotations from the Bible into the public arena in support of certain policies, many Democrats declared such behavior to be a threat to the First Amendment and to pluralism. One difference is that Republicans such as Pat Robertson used the Bible to defend the unborn and to criticize the gay rights movement.

In his acceptance speech at the Democratic Convention, Bill Clinton spoke of a "new covenant" he wanted to make with the American people. A covenant depends largely on the character of the one making it. God's character is without question. Clinton's remains to be seen. In his acceptance speech, Al Gore said, "In the words of the Bible, 'Do not lose heart. This nation will be renewed.'" No such verse appears in the Scriptures.

Both Clinton and Gore tolerate and promote abortion. The worth of unborn American citizens is established in several Bible verses, which both men ignore in their selective and sometimes inaccurate proof texting. They also see nothing wrong with homosexual practices, which are frequently condemned in the Bible.

A false or flawed theology can influence the political direction of a person and a nation. If our leaders claim to believe and order their lives according to Scripture, but misinterpret, misunderstand, or misapply biblical instructions, disaster can result (see reference no. 5).

Prov. 23:7, KJV:

*For as he thinketh in his heart, so is he: Eat and drink, saith he to thee; but his heart is not with thee.*

Is. 28:15, KJV:

*Because ye have said, We have made a covenant with death, and with hell are we at agreement; when the overflowing scourge shall pass through, it shall not come unto us: for we have made lies our refuge, and under falsehood have we hid ourselves.*

Though Clinton and Gore use the Bible as they please, they have put a gag rule on military chaplains. So far, no active-duty chaplains have been called to testify before any of the congressional committees considering the President's drive to lift the ban on homosexuals in the military. But there is little the Pentagon can do to stop retired chaplains from speaking out. James Hutchens, who was a National Guard brigadier general, said, "For the military to yield to this demand would place the government in the position of 'establishment religion'...teaching service members that their moral values, based on their religious upbringings, were wrong. But even worse would be the establishment of a politically correct religion that affirms homosexuality as morally acceptable. That, I submit, is unconstitutional" (see reference no. 29).

The gay issue in the military is explosive. Top military leaders oppose the policy change, saying that open displays of homosexuality in the military would undermine morale and discipline, and open a Pandora's box of sexual harassment actions. They also note that sharing barracks, showers, and latrines, especially in combat or at sea, could pose overwhelming logistical problems. Then there is the threat of AIDS spreading through the ranks.

General Colin Powell says that homosexual behavior is inconsistent with maintaining good order and discipline. He also does not like the comparison of discrimination against blacks with that of homosexuals. He said, "Skin color is a benign, non-behavioral characteristic. Sexual orientation is perhaps the most profound of human characteristics. Comparison of the two is a convenient but invalid argument" (see reference no. 5).

Other than child sacrifice through abortion, nothing else enflames the American people more right now than the issue over gay and lesbian rights. Our local church, Praise Tabernacle, is 15 miles north of Camp LeJeune, Jacksonville, North Carolina. We are a multi-racial, civilian-military congregation. This gay issue is unprecedented in American life and military history...and it is dangerous. Homosexuality is the strongest spirit I have ever faced as a pastor. Like Goliath, the aggressive, militant side of this demonic spirit is a loud-mouthed bully.

The sin of sodomy is not a hopeless one. Men and women snared by this spirit need to hear the good news about Jesus Christ and His forgiveness. Many are being set free and some have even been healed of AIDS. Those who deny His power are openly declaring their rebellion.

## Unnatural Affection

Hab. 1:6-7, KJV:

> *For, lo, I raise up the Chaldeans, that bitter and hasty nation, which shall march through the breadth of*

*the land, to possess the dwellingplaces that are not theirs.*

*They are terrible and dreadful: their judgment and their dignity shall proceed of themselves.*

Blatant, bold, ungodly in act and attitude, this new political lobby wants our youth to be aware of gay "rights." Their goal: to make open homosexuality a legitimate and acceptable life style in the minds of the American people. Gay activists called the 1992 presidential election their "national coming out as a political force" (see reference no. 5).

Judg. 21:25, KJV:

*In those days there was no king in Israel: every man did that which was right in his own eyes.*

Judg. 21:25, NIV:

*In those days Israel had no king; everyone did as he saw fit.*

In this age of relativism where everything, especially morals, are the private, personal whims of each man, our only hope is the Bible, the inspired Word of the living God. In spite of what the secular humanists say, there are absolutes; there are values that are right and wrong. In the light of the Scriptures, all gray areas polarize into righteousness or sin, wheat or tares, Christ or antichrist. If there is no measure, canon, or rule, then we are doomed to pluralistic anarchy. Starting with Genesis, the Book of Beginnings, we must view sodomy by going back to Sodom.

Gen. 19:5-7, NIV:

*They called to Lot, "Where are the men who came to you tonight? Bring them out to us so that we can have sex with them."*

*Lot went outside to meet them and shut the door behind him*

*and said, "No, my friends. Don't do this wicked thing."*

Lev. 18:22-23, NIV:

*Do not lie with a man as one lies with a woman; that is detestable.*

*Do not have sexual relations with an animal and defile yourself with it. A woman must not present herself to an animal to have sexual relations with it; that is a perversion.*

Lev. 20:13, NIV:

*If a man lies with a man as one lies with a woman, both of them have done what is detestable. They must be put to death; their blood will be on their own heads.*

AIDS is contaminated blood, devoid of its life-preserving power!

Deut. 23:17, KJV:

*There shall be no whore of the daughters of Israel, nor a sodomite of the sons of Israel.*

Judg. 19:22, NIV:

*While they were enjoying themselves, some of the wicked men of the city surrounded the house. Pounding* on the door, they shouted to the old man who owned the house, "Bring out the man who came to your house so we can have sex with him."

1 Kings 14:24, KJV:

*And there were also sodomites in the land: and they did according to all the abominations of the nations which the Lord cast out before the children of Israel.*

Rom. 1:24-27, NIV:

*Therefore God gave them over in the sinful desires of their hearts to sexual impurity for the degrading of their bodies with one another.*

*They exchanged the truth of God for a lie, and worshiped and served created things rather than the Creator—who is forever praised. Amen.*

*Because of this, God gave them over to shameful lusts. Even their women exchanged natural relations for unnatural ones.*

*In the same way the men also abandoned natural relations with women and were inflamed with lust for one another. Men committed indecent acts with other men, and received in themselves the due penalty for their perversion.*

Is the affliction of AIDS which men and women have received "in themselves" the due penalty for their perversion?

1 Cor. 6:9, NIV:

*Do you not know that the wicked will not inherit the kingdom of God? Do not be deceived: Neither the*

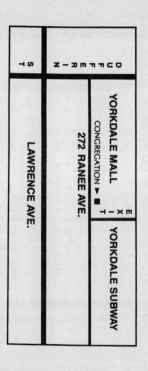

DUFFERIN ST.

YORKDALE MALL

CONGREGATION ▼ ■ EXIT

272 RANEE AVE.

YORKDALE SUBWAY

LAWRENCE AVE.

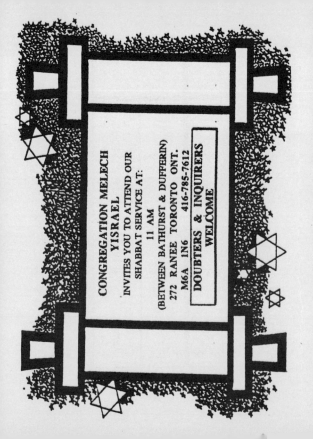

CONGREGATION MELECH
YISRAEL
INVITES YOU TO ATTEND OUR
SHABBAT SERVICE AT:
11 AM
(BETWEEN BATHURST & DUFFERIN)
272 RANEE TORONTO ONT.
M6A 1N6   416-785-7612
DOUBTERS & INQUIRERS
WELCOME

*sexually immoral nor idolaters nor adulterers nor male prostitutes nor homosexual offenders.*

1 Tim. 1:9-10, KJV:

*Knowing this, that the law is not made for a righteous man, but for the lawless and disobedient, for the ungodly and for sinners, for unholy and profane, for murderers of fathers and murderers of mothers, for manslayers,*

*For whoremongers, for them that defile themselves with mankind...*

Both Testaments are clear on the subject of homosexuality and lesbianism. Let God and His Word be true, and every man a liar (Jn. 1:1; Rom. 3:4).

The gay rights movement is not about expanding freedom; it is about circumscribing freedom. Its agenda demands that any employer, landlord, or home seller who acts on his belief that sodomy is unnatural and morally wrong be exposed, prosecuted, punished, and branded a bigot. Gay rights wants the power of government behind its minority view. For example, the Boy Scouts of America believe homosexuals are a poor example and a potential danger to boys in their custody. Gay rights wants the Boy Scouts punished with a loss of contributions until the Scouts permit homosexuals to become scoutmasters (see reference no. 15).

One of scouts notable persecutors has been Roberta Achtenburg, a militant lesbian activist, supporter of ACT-UP (a radical gay organization), and now Assistant Secretary of HUD, Housing and Urban Development. In charge of "fair" housing, HUD will encourage homosexuals and lesbians to move into government neighborhoods and possibly mandate quotas. The Scouts are out and the gays are in (see reference no. 15).

The gay strategy is to undermine the Church and desensitize Americans. They portray conservative Christianity as antiquated backwaters, badly out of step with the times and with the latest findings of psychology. They know that they will never persuade the masses that homosexuality is a "good" thing, but just "another" thing. They want us to view sodomy with indifference instead of with keen emotion. But there is nothing passive about their demands:

1. *A "civil rights" bill for their "persecuted" minority.*
2. *The repeal of all sodomy laws.*
3. *The redefining of the family, including gay "marriages."*
4. *The adoption of children by gay couples.*
5. *Gay curricula and teachers in the public schools.*
6. *Multiple partner "unions."*
7. *The training of servicemen and chaplains to accept gays in the military* (see reference no. 17).

There are people in the extremes of gay activism who are saying, "If you don't give us what we want, we are going to contaminate the blood supply. We are going to declare war!" How would you (or your child or grandchild) like to go to the hospital, needing blood, and knowing that there are demonized people in America who would kill you just to parade their flesh?

Homosexual and lesbian organizations gave over 2.5 million dollars to the election campaign of Bill Clinton.

Now they want action for their money and their votes. *The Washington Blade*, D.C.'s gay newspaper, has reported that one of the President's first priorities will be to pass laws that will force Christian churches, schools, and organizations to hire homosexual pastors or other personnel, or face severe penalties in lawsuits (see reference no. 17).

There is evidence in Washington of growing official acceptance of the homosexual life style. Congressional sponsorship of the federal gay and lesbian rights bill has increased to 109 in the House and 17 in the Senate, compared to 73 in the house and 6 in the Senate just six years ago. And the number of openly homosexual elected and appointed officials in government has grown to 85 (see reference no. 15).

The gay-lesbian issue is bigger than most folks think. Several well-known groups endorsed the recent homosexual march in Washington. Included were the NAACP, National Organization for Women, American Civil Liberties Union, Southern Christian Leadership Conference, People for the American Way, Unitarian Universalists Association of Congregations, United Church of Christ office for Church in Society, Union of American Hebrew Congregations, World Congress of Gay and Lesbian Jewish Organizations, SIECUS—Sex Information and Education Council of the U.S., and the American Humanist Association (see reference no. 17).

The militant homosexual rights lobby mustered between 100,000 and 300,000 supporters (rather than the advanced billing of a million) to their "Lesbian, Gay and Bi-Equal Rights and Liberation March" in April of 1993.

The figures were less embarrassing than the X-rated performances of some of the participants and entertainment
stars. Even politicians ran from the event, and President
Clinton himself arranged to be out of town. Jesse Jackson, never a stranger to a microphone, was an exception.
So were the only openly homosexual members of Congress, Democratic Representatives Barney Frank and
Gerry Studds, both of Massachusetts. Frank's letter in the
program guide was signed by himself and his "spouse,"
Herb Moses (see reference no. 15).

Yet a new national study of male sexual behavior shows
that about 2 percent of men surveyed had engaged in
homosexual sex and only 1 percent considered themselves exclusively homosexual. The figures in the study
released by the Alan Guttmacher Institute are significantly lower than the 10 percent figure that has been
part of the country's conventional wisdom since it was
published in the Kinsey report more than four decades
ago (see reference no. 17).

Some are standing up in America. Mary Cummins,
the grandmother who thrashed city hall, was appalled
by the notorious "Children of the Rainbow" curriculum.
Mrs. Cummins, president of New York District 24 school
board (Queens) refused to use the curriculum of New
York City Schools Chancellor Joseph Fernandez. It man-
dated that teachers introduce the propaganda of activist
homosexuals into every elementary grade—first through
eighth—and into every class, no matter what the subject.
Fernandez shocked the city by suspending the entire
nine-member board. Later, the New York City Board of
Education reversed that decision by a unanimous vote of

6-0. Books like *Daddy's Roommate* and *Heather Has Two Mommies* encouraged children to view gays and lesbians as real people to be respected and appreciated (see reference no. 15).

The gay/lesbian life style has a price that goes with it. In days of inflation, the wages of sin is still death. In fact, it's costing all of us. Before Clinton hiked AIDS funding in his new budget, the government was spending $15,450 per AIDS patient, compared to $285 per cancer patient, $33 per heart patient, and $25 per diabetes patient. Almost 60 percent of the AIDS cases in the U.S. are homosexual men, and their life style is directly linked to the spread of the disease. The AIDS epidemic is wiping out the male homosexual community, which explains why they are targeting the youth of America through the educational system. The life span of the average male homosexual is around 40 years (see reference no. 15).

How far has this perversion gone? Prominent homosexual leaders and publications have voiced support for pedophilia, incest, sadomasochism, and even bestiality (see reference no. 17).

Ex. 22:19, NIV:

*Anyone who has sexual relations with an animal must be put to death.*

According to *The Washington Blade*, the city's weekly homosexual publication, lesbian couples are learning to bear children by means of "alternative" insemination. The donor is either chosen or anonymous, and many women are inseminating their partner at home. Most of the children will never know the name of their father (see reference no. 5).

The homosexual agenda continues to maintain its stronghold on prime-time television. It is clearly a priority of the networks to offer "politically correct" perspectives and gently guide Americans into a new tolerance. Young children are unable to distinguish fact from fantasy; they regard television as information about how the world works. The February 2nd, 1993 episode of ABC's *The Jackie Thomas Show* had a pro-homosexual theme. The executive producers of the series are Tom and Roseanne Arnold. The Fox network's *Melrose Place* is explicitly pro-gay. There continues a startling escalation of illicit immorality in prime-time "family" shows (see reference no. 17).

Also, CBS/Fox Video, leading an unprecedented charge into the gay market, has announced a national "mobilization" campaign to launch the homosexual-promoting film *The Lost Language of the Cranes*. Sal Scamardo, director of promotions, said, "We know demand's there for gay and lesbian titles all over the country, not just in New York and San Francisco...Our ultimate goal is to better serve gay and lesbian consumers by integrating titles that speak to them into more stores in more places." CBS/Fox will also donate a portion of rental receipts to VIAC, the Video Industry AIDS Coalition (see reference no. 17).

The Chaldeans ridiculed strongholds. So has the homosexual novelist Gore Vidal. His latest book, *Live From Golgotha*, released by Random House, twists the Gospel account by having Judas crucified in the place of Jesus Christ. It also portrays Paul and Timothy as homosexual lovers. Vidal has said that he believes Christianity to be "the greatest disaster ever to befall the West" (see reference no. 5).

Rom. 1:28-32, NIV:

*Furthermore, since they did not think it worthwhile to retain the knowledge of God, He gave them over to a depraved mind, to do what ought not to be done.*

*They have become filled with every kind of wickedness, evil, greed and depravity. They are full of envy, murder, strife, deceit and malice. They are gossips,*

*slanderers, God-haters, insolent, arrogant and boastful; they invent ways of doing evil; they disobey their parents;*

*they are senseless, faithless, heartless, ruthless.*

*Although they know God's righteous decree that those who do such things deserve death, they not only continue to do these very things but also approve of those who practice them.*

Gal. 6:7-8, NIV:

*Do not be deceived: God cannot be mocked. A man reaps what he sows.*

*The one who sows to please his sinful nature, from that nature will reap destruction; the one who sows to please the Spirit, from the Spirit will reap eternal life.*

Eph. 5:11-16, NIV:

*Have nothing to do with the fruitless deeds of darkness, but rather expose them.*

*For it is shameful even to mention what the dis-
obedient do in secret.*

*But everything exposed by the light becomes visible,*

*for it is light that makes everything visible. This is
why it is said: "Wake up, O sleeper, rise from the dead,
and Christ will shine on you."*

*Be very careful, then, how you live—not as unwise
but as wise,*

*making the most of every opportunity, because the
days are evil.*

### History Repeats Itself

Child sacrifice and sodomy were the norm during the
administration of King Jehoiakim over 2,500 years ago.
Judah in Habakkuk's day is America today.

A more recent example of history repeating itself is
the present administration's rehashing of the days of
Jimmy Carter. The information below is detailed, but
necessary to know in our present day of trouble.

In Carter's day, Hamilton Jordan, his brilliant but socially obnoxious campaign manager said, "If, after the inauguration you find Cy Vance as Secretary of State and
Zbigniew Brezinski as head of national security, then I
would say that we failed, and I'd quit." But, in fact, that is
precisely what happened. Carter's teacher, Brezinski, took
the National Security Council post. Cyrus Vance, who had
previously served as president of the Rockefeller Foundation (as had Dean Rusk), was made Secretary of State.

Trilateral Commission member Walter Mondale,
whose brother had signed the first Humanist Manifesto,

was selected as Carter's Vice President. Council on Foreign Relations member Stansfield Turner was placed in charge of the CIA. Trilateral member Mike Blumenthal was put in charge of the treasury. Paul Volcker, a former employee of Rockefeller's Chase Manhattan Bank, was given the powerful role of chairman of the Federal Reserve Board. Out of only 65 American members on the Trilateral Commission, 13 of them, including the President and Vice President, were given top posts in the Carter administration (see reference no. 23).

Bill Clinton won the presidency in '92 by claiming not to be a liberal but a "New Democrat." With the assistance of his willing accomplices, the liberal media, he sold his line to the American public. Not liberal? Bigger government, the redistribution of taxes, the exploitation of class envy, the desensitizing of public mores while rationalizing special interests' private agenda—this is the "New Democrat"? Moreover, what about some of his cabinet-level appointments? How do they fit into his "new covenant"?

Les Aspin, Jr., Secretary of Defense, has served in Congress for the past 22 years. He has said he plans to carry out Clinton's promise to lift the ban on gays in the military. Warren Christopher, Secretary of State, established his diplomatic credentials under Cyrus Vance in the Carter administration. Janet Reno, Attorney General, is opposed to capital punishment. Richard W. Riley, Secretary of Education, adamantly opposes school choice. Lloyd Bentsen, Secretary of the Treasury, has been a Democratic senator from Texas since 1970. Dr. Joycelyn Elders, U.S. Surgeon General, is pro-abortion. She has said that she will advocate the medicinal use of marijuana and has promised to continue her support for distributing condoms from high school-based clinics (see reference no. 5).

Anthony Lake, the national security adviser, worked for Presidents Kennedy and Nixon, was the director of policy planning in Carter's State Department, and was always close to Henry Kissinger and Cyrus Vance. James Woolsey, director of the CIA, was undersecretary of the Navy from 1977-79 in the Carter administration. Madeleine Albright, ambassador to the U.N., has worked on several Democratic campaigns, including those of former Senator Edmund Muskie, 1984 vice-presidential candidate Geraldine Ferraro, and 1988 presidential nominee Michael Dukakis. Bill Clinton elevated her post to cabinet level. Samuel Berger, deputy director of the National Security Council, was the deputy director of the State Department's policy planning during the Carter administration. Hazel O'Leary, the energy secretary, was appointed to federal energy posts by both Presidents Gerald Ford and Carter (see reference no. 5).

Let's take a closer look at four of these partners in Clinton's "new" Democratic administration—the Secretary of Defense, the Secretary of State, the Attorney General, and the Secretary of the Treasury.

Les Aspin, Jr., Secretary of Defense, graduated from Yale, Oxford, and MIT. He studied at the feet of Robert McNamara in the McNamara-Kennedy-Johnson Pentagon. This former head of the House Armed Services Committee served his own military tour far from the front lines, not as a "grunt" but as an economist in the Pentagon. He supports (along with Hillary Clinton and Derek

Shearer) the Institute for Policy Studies, a Marxist think tank which the FBI has accused of being funded by the KGB (see reference no. 6).

With all the unproven allegations about the Reagan administration having attempted to trade arms for hostages, it now turns out that it was Warren Christopher (now Secretary of State) in the Carter administration who attempted to swap millions in military equipment, along with billions of dollars in frozen Iranian assets, for the hostages in Tehran! A strong proponent of a new world order and part of a law firm with international interests (though our new President protested the influence of lobbyists who work for foreign interests), Christopher's first comment after his nomination was, "We face a world where borders matter less and less..." (see reference no. 6).

In Habakkuk's day, justice was perverted and the court system crippled. Janet Reno is Bill Clinton's new Attorney General. Never married and childless, she is pro-choice on abortion. She was brought to Clinton's attention by Hugh Rodham, Hillary's brother. Some have dubbed Hillary and Janet as "soul sisters." Reno is Harvard-educated and loved by feminists. Patricia Ireland, Miami lawyer and head of the National Organization for Women, is a long-time supporter. Christian and conservative groups in Florida have called Reno soft on crime, especially pornography. She has stated, "My highest priority is to protect the rights of the guilty, not to convict the guilty" (see reference no. 6).

Lloyd Bentsen, the new Secretary of the Treasury, a multimillionaire Texan, was the unsuccessful candidate for Vice President in 1988. He resigned his politically incorrect tennis and country clubs since they were not all-inclusive, then rejoined after the campaign failed. He is ranked by the National Taxpayer's Union as among the biggest spenders in Congress (see reference no. 6).

We must conclude that the "newness" of the present administration is not so new.

But President Clinton still needs a "new" package to wrap it all in. Enter the media, the biased media. With its help, the current administration is rewriting history, reminding us constantly of "the past 12 years" under Reagan and Bush. The fact is that revenues during the Reagan years doubled. In spite of this, a liberal congress continued to overspend. Let's tell the whole story, gentlemen (see reference no. 22).

Many key media people are past or present members of the Council on Foreign Relations and the Trilateral Commission: Dan Rather and Harry Reasoner from CBS, David Brinkley and John Chancellor from NBC, Ted Koppel and Barbara Walters from ABC, as well as key people for *Time* and *Newsweek* (see reference no. 12).

Consider this: When Bill Clinton had yet to hold a single news conference a full month after his inauguration, ABC News—in a two-hour special hosted by Peter Jennings—allowed Clinton to answer softball questions from the kiddie corps. The damage to the network's reputation was compounded the next day when *The New York Times* not only revealed that questions for the President had been scripted and rehearsed in advance, but also caught the network in an apparent falsehood designed to cover up the collusion that had occurred between program producers and Clinton representatives (see reference no. 15).

Several surveys over the past decade have proven that members of the media are generally far more liberal and/or are Democrats than the population at large. Their personal views certainly impact their coverage of the news. The Newspaper Association of America (NAA) commissioned a poll of 94 editors, 89 publishers, and 22 executives carrying both titles. The NAA asked, "Do you believe there's bias in the general media's political coverage?" Yes, responded a slight majority of 51.7 percent. Those who responded affirmatively were then asked "toward which agenda, conservative or liberal?" A whopping 70.8 percent said liberal. Just 7.5 percent said conservative (see reference no. 20).

It should come as no surprise that the media is biased against Christian values in serving up its daily fare. America is no longer a Christian nation. We must return to the Lord.

Although abortion and sodomy are abominable in God's sight, they (and all sinful acts of men) flow from Judah's and America's biggest, basic problem: idolatry!

### Mother Earth, Not Father God

Hab. 2:18, NIV:

*Of what value is an idol, since a man has carved it? Or an image that teaches lies? For he who makes it trusts in his own creation; he makes idols that cannot speak.*

Ex. 20:3-5, NIV:

*You shall have no other gods before Me.*

*You shall not make for yourself an idol in the form of anything in heaven above or on the earth beneath or in the waters below.*

*You shall not bow down to them or worship them; for I, the Lord your God, am a jealous God, punishing the children for the sin of the fathers to the third and fourth generation of those who hate Me....*

Acts 17:22-23, NIV:

*Paul then stood up in the meeting of the Areopagus and said: "Men of Athens! I see that in every way you are very religious.*

*For as I walked around and looked carefully at your objects of worship, I even found an altar with this inscription: TO AN UNKNOWN GOD. Now what you worship as something unknown I am going to proclaim to you.*

Acts 17:29, NIV:

*Therefore since we are God's offspring, we should not think that the divine being is like gold or silver or stone—an image made by man's design and skill.*

Rom. 1:22-25, NIV:

*Although they claimed to be wise, they became fools*

*and exchanged the glory of the immortal God for images made to look like mortal man and birds and animals and reptiles.*

*Therefore God gave them over in the sinful desires of their hearts to sexual impurity for the degrading of their bodies with one another.*

*They exchanged the truth of God for a lie, and worshiped and served created things rather than the Creator—who is forever praised. Amen.*

In Habakkuk's day, idolatry was Judah's primary sin. Both Jeremiah and Ezekiel had warned her not to follow the example of Israel, the northern kingdom, which had reaped what she had sowed and was carried away captive by the Assyrians in 722 B.C. The southern kingdom and the inhabitants of Jerusalem refused to listen to the pleadings of the prophets. Their demise was detailed in the preceding chapter.

Idolatry comes in many forms. America was given to it long before Bill Clinton got into office or the New Agers became so prominent. There is a difference between Christianity and religion. Christianity is a living, personal relationship with Jesus Christ, God Almighty. Religion is a mixture of what men and demons teach.

In 1986, Pope John Paul II joined in a circle to pray and meditate with snake handlers from Togo, shamans and tribal witchdoctors from West Africa, Hindu gurus from India, Buddhist monks from Thailand, and liberal Protestant clergymen from Great Britain. He later said, "There are many paths to God." In January of 1993, the Pope again hosted the Dalai Lama of Tibetan Buddhism and representatives of many other religions. In February, one month later, he met in Benin, Africa, with voodoo believers and sorcerers, suggesting that they would not betray their traditional faith by converting to Christianity (see reference no. 11).

Polytheism is the worship of many gods. Pantheism believes that everything is god and includes the worship of Mother Nature. Open idolatry and paganism is obvious. The religion of the New Agers is more subtle.

During the inaugural ceremony for President Clinton, poet Maya Angelou arose to give an original reading. Angelou, a darling of the New Age crowd, wowed an international TV audience with dreamy, spiritually-oriented lyrics that had human beings talking to rocks, trees, forests, and rivers. It was touching and sensitive if one is heavy into environmentalism, crystals, the worship of Mother Earth, and Hindu pantheism. She is a church-goer, however, although it doesn't seem to matter what kind, having frequented Moslem mosques, Jewish synagogues, Buddhist temples, and pro-gay churches all with equal enthusiasm (see reference no. 11).

Vice President Gore is known for being a leader and author in the environmentalism field, having written *Earth in the Balance*. Environmental concerns are now driving public policy as never before. EPA regulations cost a lot of money, some $123 billion annually, and that figure will rise to more than $200 billion by the year 2000.

We need to take another look at many of the doomsday predictions of the earth worshipers. This may even steal the thunder of some hyper-dispensationalists who deem themselves eschatological experts (men without the Holy Ghost are ever harping on something to "scare" people to Christ before it's "too late"). There is increasing scientific evidence that the earth and its inhabitants may be here for a while (see reference no. 15).

The sky is falling on radical environmentalism, the worship of Mother Nature. Looking at a few "enviro-facts," we learn that every American could fit into Texas with a three-acre tract per family of four. The entire world's population could be put into Alaska, California, and Texas with each person enjoying more than one tenth acre of land. The garbage that Americans produce for the next 1,000 years would fit into an area 44 miles square and 120 feet deep (about half of one percent of our land). Landfill shortages result from shortages in common sense and surpluses of harebrained public policy—not from shortages of land.

Since communism has lost respectability, environmentalism has become the new attack against capitalism. In its quest for control, the red-turned-green communist agenda calls for lies and half-truths to create mass panic (see reference no. 5).

For example, the spotted owl controversy has devastated the Pacific Northwest. In Happy Camp, California (a microcosm of the regional situation), environmental regulations have produced a 60 percent drop in local employment. The timber harvest in four national forests has been slashed by 85 percent. Family members are being scattered as breadwinners are forced to relocate. This has resulted in an increase in juvenile crime, spousal abuse, and divorce. Sadder still is that Native Americans play a major role in the western timber industry. The government violated the original Indian treaty by never paying them for their land, and now is starving them out over a dumb bird (see reference no. 15).

Animal rights are more important to pantheists than human rights. Humanists abort over a million and a half unborn American citizens every year and say nothing; let a lower species be "endangered," and they scream, "Murder!"

In 1973, Congress passed the Endangered Species Act, which was designed to save wildlife in danger of extinction. Twenty years later, environmental bureauocrats are using the law to violate citizens' civil rights and take away personal property without just compensation. Once a species is listed, it is a federal crime to kill that animal, and restrictions are placed on any property that might be home for the species.

In Texas, a man killed an endangered whooping crane and was imprisoned for six months and fined over $200,000. Meanwhile, killers, rapists, and drug dealers go free on technicalities. As in Habakkuk's day, the law is "crippled" and justice rarely goes forth. An elderly couple in Georgia, needing money for medical expenses, tried to sell some timber on their land. They were stopped by the government because a red cockaded woodpecker might live there, despite the fact that none had been sighted for years.

The reason the Green Movement has such a veneration for old growth forests is because they worship nature rather than God. This is Hinduism repackaged for the West, believing that nature is perfect until man disfigures it, and that if left alone, nature will return to perfection. Extremists believe that phasing out the human race will solve every problem on earth, social and environmental (see reference no. 5).

Acts 17:30, NIV:

*In the past God overlooked such ignorance, but now He commands all people everywhere to repent.*

The worship of Mother Nature is but one example of idolatry in America. We need not belabor the point. God judged

Judah for her idolatry. The Day of the Lord has dawned in this nation. We must forsake every idol, every false image. The apostle Paul called them vain imaginations (2 Cor. 10:3-6). We must again become one nation under one God. There is only one true God. His name is Jesus.

Mt. 1:21, KJV:

*And she shall bring forth a Son, and thou shalt call his name JESUS: for He shall save His people from their sins.*

Acts 4:12, NIV:

*Salvation is found in no one else, for there is no other name under heaven given to men by which we must be saved.*

Phil. 2:8-11, NIV:

*And being found in appearance as a man, He humbled Himself and became obedient to death—even death on a cross!*

*Therefore God exalted Him to the highest place and gave Him the name that is above every name,*

*that at the name of Jesus every knee should bow, in heaven and on earth and under the earth,*

*and every tongue confess that Jesus Christ is Lord, to the glory of God the Father.*

### Bits and Pieces

Hab. 1:10, KJV:

*And they shall scoff at the kings, and the princes shall be a scorn unto them: they shall deride every strong hold; for they shall heap dust, and take it.*

"They shall deride every stronghold," every moral value and biblical principle upon which this great nation was founded. Chaldeans, past and present, mock all authority, especially spiritual authority. Jesus Christ as King and Lord is not at all in their thoughts.

In Habakkuk's time, Judah was filled with injustice and wickedness. It is a powerful picture of America in the 1990s. This chapter could have been expanded and published as a separate volume. Because that may yet happen (and because focusing on America's sinful condition is wearisome), we will conclude at this point with some "bits and pieces." Just as the last five chapters of the Book of Judges reveal daily life in a time when everyone "did his own thing," consider the things that are happening now in America.

The early 1993 terrorist bombing in New York City got everybody thinking. The State Department finally conceded in April of 1993 that the Egyptian government had been warning the U.S. for months about the danger posed by Sheik Omar Abdel Rahman and his fundamentalist agitation in New Jersey. This man is believed to be responsible for the bombings (see reference no. 22).

Armand Hammer, convicted felon, died in 1990. He was a devoted Marxist revolutionary who did everything in his power to aid and abet the communist butchers in Russia and the communist party in America. He was also a very rich man, the head of Occidental Petroleum, and the "Daddy Warbucks" of Albert Gore, Jr., our new Vice President. In the 1920s, Hammer became a follower of Lenin. He met privately over the years with Stalin, Khrushchev, Brezhnev, and finally, Gorbachev.

Pardoned by George Bush in 1989, the communist bagman, the Marxist millionaire, feathered the nests of Presidents Roosevelt, Nixon, and Bush, Senator Al Gore Sr., and now Vice President Al Gore, Jr. (see reference no. 11).

Why has the number of rapes risen to such gigantic proportions? What factors are now common in today's society that were not in yesterday's? For one thing, pornography is everywhere. Television, radio, billboards, fashion clothing, and magazines all use explicit sex to attract attention. Books, films, and music exploiting sex are available to almost anyone. Even in our schools, where sex education is taught without moral backing, prurient literature is made available by teachers while God's Word and the mention of God have been banned. We give children poison but withhold the antidote (see reference no. 17).

Six out of ten new marriages are failing and many of the rest are unhappy. Divorce is a scourge, having tripled since 1960, from 393,000 to 1,187,000 in 1991. Co-habitation has increased sixfold since 1960 and now precedes the majority of marriages in America. Sadly, most churches are only "blessing machines," preparing couples for weddings, not lifelong marriages. Less than 20 percent of marriages have premarital counseling. God expects parents to train their children in the ways of the Lord; however, only 15 percent of mothers and 8 percent of fathers have ever talked to their children about premarital sex (see refrence no. 17).

Michael Medved, commenting on Hollywood and today's movies, said, "One reason the industry has become so left-wing is, I think, because to get to a position of power you have to largely cut yourself off from normal ties of family, church or synagogue, and community. You become a rootless, cutthroat technocrat...To succeed in this business—and that's one of the reasons I left working as screenwriter—you must be completely driven and obsessed" (see reference no. 19).

Peter Marshall, author of *The Light and the Glory*, shows that our schools are leaving out the Christian heritage part of American history. He said, "The last three generations of Americans simply have not been told the truth...the history books began to be rewritten in the 20s and the 30s...what we call revisionist history. Words like duty and honor and country fell very much out of vogue, and the stories of the Christian faith...were simply left out. And consequently we've had the teachers who were themselves educated in the 20s and 30s... who did not know these things. You can't teach what you don't know" (see reference no. 5).

As they were protesting national drug policies and supposedly overly harsh sentencing guidelines, two prominent New York City federal judges announced that they would no longer preside over drug cases (see reference no. 15).

Oliver North recently said, "Everybody wishes Bill Clinton well as President of the United States. But we have to be realistic: Our country is entering into a very dangerous period...A man is about to assume the Oval Office who has no foreign policy experience at all" (see reference no. 5).

In 1940, Americans paid 3 percent of their incomes in personal taxes. Federal spending, 15 percent of the Gross

Domestic Product by 1950, is now 25 percent and rising, and the average family is working until May 5th just to earn enough money to pay their taxes (see reference no. 15).

In 1988, Democratic presidential candidate Michael Dukakis was politically wounded when he admitted he was a "card-carrying" member of the American Civil Liberties Union. But in 1993, the ACLU is "in." Harvard University vice-president John Shattuck and Morton Halperin, both of whom have held high positions with this far-left organization, are now going to hold high positions in the federal government as well, enabling them to shape U.S. foreign and defense policy. Not only is their ideology virtually certain to drive them into urging U.S. support for leftist movements and governments around the globe, but judging from their own statements on national security, they clearly cannot be trusted with the most sensitive military and diplomatic secrets to which they are certain to be privy (see reference no. 15).

American government has far outgrown the limits set by our founders in the Constitution. If the twenty-first century is to be the American century, government must be redirected to its proper and legitimate role. The growth of government is the greatest tragedy of the twentieth century (see reference no. 14).

That is enough. It wearies me. Anyone can see that America is facing the day of trouble. Many believe that all these things are not just happening, but are part of some great, sinister master plan.

## Is There a Conspiracy?

Conspiracies and confederations by the enemies of the Lord are found throughout the Bible: Canaanite

kings joined hands against Joshua (Josh. 10); mixed multitudes conspired against Nehemiah's project of rebuild-
ing the wall and gates of Jerusalem (Neh. 4-6); religious
leaders plotted Jesus' execution (Mt. 26:1-16). These
same men then tried to frustrate the apostles of the early
Church (Acts 4).

Is there a conspiracy going on in America? It's possible.

To some, the term "the Insiders" does not refer to those
who break the law, but to the people who make the law,
nationally and internationally. These elitists occupy the
highest councils of government, the media, banking, big
business, education, and the major tax-free foundations.
No exclusive clubs are as important as two private, secre-
tive, by-invitation-only organizations that are based in
New York City—the Council of Foreign Relations and
the Trilateral Commission.

The CFR was founded in 1921 by a small group of in-
ternationalists. It is the largest American group of "Insiders" working to create what they have long described
as a "New World Order." Some believe it to be the "front
organization" for the heart of the American Establishment. The CFR has about 2,900 members.

The Trilateral Commission was founded in 1973 by
David Rockefeller to bring together key governmental
officials and private leaders from Europe, Japan, and the
United States. There are about 75 American members of
the Trilateral Commission. Significantly, Bill Clinton has
been a member of both the CFR and the TLC for years
(see reference no. 6).

King Jehoiakim of Judah was nothing more than a
puppet-king, a vassal first of Egypt and then Babylon.
The only power he had was the power given him by his
benefactors. Is Bill Clinton like Jehoiakim?

Some feel that Clinton's mentor, the late Dr. Carroll Quigley, history professor from Georgetown University, and his massive work, *Tragedy and Hope,* form the ideological base for Clinton's "new covenant" and the political "conspiracy" it represents (see reference no. 6).

Is there a conspiracy? If so, the heart of its appeal is not a revolutionary new idea. It's the same old idea that the serpent whispered to Eve: "Ye shall be as gods..." (Gen. 3:5b, KJV).

Men live by ideas, and no idea in man's history has produced more evil than this one: Man, the god. Man, the predestinate. Man, the central planner. Man, the director of the evolutionary process. Man, the maker and shaker of things on earth and in the heavens. As Marx's partner, Frederick Engels, put it over a century ago, "...man no longer proposes, but also disposes." But most important of all is this promise: Man, the savior of man (see reference no. 3).

Is there a conspiracy? I don't know. But I do know that one could be overwhelmed by focusing on the facts reported in this chapter. There's no life in that. I wrote this book to help you and your family be able to rest in the day of trouble. Let the Psalmist encourage us all:

Ps. 2:1-6, KJV:

*Why do the heathen rage, and the people imagine a vain thing?*

*The kings of the earth set themselves, and the rulers take counsel together, against the Lord, and against His anointed, saying,*

*Let us break their bands asunder, and cast away their cords from us.*

*He that sitteth in the heavens shall laugh: the Lord shall have them in derision.*

*Then shall He speak unto them in His wrath, and vex them in His sore displeasure.*

*Yet have I set My King upon My holy hill of Zion.*

Dan. 2:44, KJV:

*And in the days of these kings shall the God of heaven set up a kingdom, which shall never be destroyed: and the kingdom shall not be left to other people, but it shall break in pieces and consume all these kingdoms, and it shall stand for ever.*

Is there a conspiracy? It doesn't matter, because Jesus is King in Zion!

This is a sad day for America. Violence, iniquity, and malice are everywhere. Spoiling, strife, and contention fill our homes and spill into our streets. Our court systems are paralyzed and justice rarely goes forth. The wicked seem to surround the righteous.

Doesn't a sovereign God see all this? How long must we wait for things to change? Why doesn't the Lord do something about it? Doesn't He care what happens to America? Is there hope?

We have a problem. So did the prophet Habakkuk. Let's begin our journey by sobbing with him.

How long? Why?

### Recommended Reference Material

1. *America: To Pray or not to Pray* by David Barton, Wallbuilder Press, Aledo, TX, 1991 (book).

2. *The American Spectator*, P.O. Box 549, Arlington, VA 22216-0549 (weekly).

3. *Call it Conspiracy* by Larry Abraham, Double A Publications, P.O. Box 609, Wauna, WA 98395 (book).

4. *Chart Analysis Unlimited*, David Fuller, 7 Swallow Street, London, England WIR 7HD, Phone 011-4471734-7174 (book).

5. *Christian American*, the Christian Coalition, 1801-L Sara Drive, Chesapeake, VA 23320 (monthly except June, August, and December).

6. *The Clinton Clique* by Larry Abraham with William P. Hoar, Soundview Publications, Suite 100, 1350 Center Drive, Dunwoody, GA 30338 (book).

7. *The Closing of the American Heart* by Ronald H. Nash, Probe Ministries International, 1990 (book).

8. *Conservative Chronicle*, Box 11297, Des Moines, IA 50340-1297 (weekly).

9. *Defending the Declaration* by Gary T. Amos, Wolgemuth and Hyatt, Publishers, Inc., Brentwood, TN, 1989 (book).

10. *The Devaluing of America* by William J. Bennett, Summit Books, 1992 (book).

11. *Flashpoint*, Living Truth Ministries, Texe Marrs, 1708 Patterson Rd., Austin, TX 78733-6507.

12. *F.R.E.E.*, 1807 Columbus Avenue, Box 8616, Waco, TX 76710 (charts).

13. *Free American*, Freedom Alliance, P.O. Box 96700, Washington, D.C. 20090 (monthly).

14. *Freeman*, Foundation for Economic Education, Irving-on-Hudson, NY 10533 (monthly).

15. *Human Events*, 422 First St., S.E., Washington, D.C. 20003 (weekly).

16. *Index of Leading Cultural Indicators* by William Bennett, Heritage Foundation, 214 Massachusetts Avenue, N.E., Washington, D.C. 20002 (booklet).

17. *Journal of the American Family Association*, P.O. Drawer 2440, Tupelo, MS 38803 (monthly).

18. *The Judeo-Christian Tradition* by Dr. Gary North, P.O. Box 7999, Tyler, TX 75711 (book; many other materials).

19. *Limbaugh Letter*, EFM Publishing Inc., 342 Madison Ave., Suite 920, New York, NY 10173 (monthly).

20. *Media Watch*, Media Research Center, 113 South West St., Alexandria, VA 22314 (monthly).

21. *The Myth of Separation* by David Barton, Wallbuilder Press, Aledo, TX, 1992 (book).

22. *National Review*, 150 E. 35th St., New York, NY 10016 (bi-weekly).

23. *The New World Order* by Pat Robertson, Word Publishing, Dallas, Texas (book).

24. Omega Publications, James McKeever, P.O. Box 4130, Medford, OR 97501 (many materials).

25. *Rapid Debt Reduction Strategies* by John Avanzini, HIS Publishing Company, P.O. Box 1057, Hurst, TX 76053 (many books).

26. *Religious Rights Watch*, Christian Coalition, P.O. Box 1990, Chesapeake, VA 23327 (monthly).

27. *Ruff Times*, Howard Ruff, Editor, Target, Inc., 4457 Willow Road, Pleasanton, CA 94566, Phone 415-463-2200 (newsletter).

28. *The Spotlight*, Cordite Fidelity, Inc., 300 Independence Ave., S.E., Washington, D.C. 20003 (weekly).

29. *World*, God's World Publishing, P.O. Box 2330, Asheville, N.C. 28802 (weekly except bi-weekly in May, June, July, August, and December).

# PART ONE:
# THE BURDEN

**Sobbing Faith**

# Chapter Three

# The Problem

## "How long? Why?"

## Habakkuk 1:1-4

Hab. 1:1-4, KJV:

> *The burden which Habakkuk the prophet did see.*
>
> *O Lord, how long shall I cry, and Thou wilt not hear! even cry out unto Thee of violence, and Thou wilt not save!*
>
> *Why dost Thou shew me iniquity, and cause me to behold grievance? for spoiling and violence are before me: and there are that raise up strife and contention.*
>
> *Therefore the law is slacked, and judgment doth never go forth: for the wicked doth compass about the righteous; therefore wrong judgment proceedeth.*

Hab. 1:1, Concordant Version:

> *The load which Habakkuk the prophet perceived.*

Habakkuk had a *problem*. The Bible calls it a "burden," literally a "load, that which is lifted up" (Num. 11:11,17).

In Proverbs 30:1 and 31:1, this word is translated "prophecy"—the burden of the Lord.

Our central figure is called "the prophet" in Habakkuk 1:1 and 3:1. This is the Hebrew word *nâbîy'* (nawbee) which means "a prophet or inspired man." It comes from a root word which means "to speak or sing by inspiration." It is first used in First Samuel 10:6 to describe the function of a true prophet as he, under the influence of the divine Spirit, speaks God's message to men. The word for "see" means "to gaze at; to perceive or contemplate; to have a vision of." Compare its usage in Psalms 17:15; 27:4; 46:8; 63:2; Isaiah 33:17; and Daniel 7:9.

A prophet is one who "sees" into the realm of the Spirit and then speaks for God, revealing God unto men. Habakkuk had this kind of prophetic commission. In America and around the world, there is arising a prophetic people who have been deeply stirred to call upon the name of the Lord. They have been ordained of the Lord to speak His present purposes to this generation.

Our nation is in trouble. The previous chapter drew a parallel between this day and that of the ancient prophet. Times haven't really changed. The root of the problem is the same: the condition of the human heart. It must be converted and turned to the Lord. God's Kingdom is to be over every other. There is only one true God.

As Judah did with Molech and Chemosh, the heathen gods of Ammon and Moab, we have turned our children over to idols. This nation is guilty of murdering its unborn and throwing its young into the consuming fire of humanistic compromise. We have sacrificed our heritage, and sold our future.

Nothing much seems to make sense. A death-like shroud of futility, a sense of hopelessness, has draped itself over the land of the free and the home of the brave. People are crazy. The nations are mad.

When will it all stop? Does anybody know? Does anybody care? With Habakkuk we cry, "God, do You care?"

So we groan. Not satisfied, our reason raises the second question.

### Why?

Hab. 1:3, KJV:

*Why dost Thou shew me iniquity, and cause me to behold grievance? for spoiling and violence are before me: and there are that raise up strife and contention.*

Hab. 1:3, TLB:

*Must I forever see this sin and sadness all around me? Wherever I look I see oppression and bribery and men who love to argue and to fight.*

The words used by the prophet here reveal much about Judah then and America now. Like Ezekiel, his contemporary in Babylon prophesying to those already exiled, Habakkuk saw these things by the Spirit. It all points to the domestic oppression of America in the 90s.

The word for "iniquity" means "nothingness, vanity, an idol." The word for "grievance" means "toil, a wearing effect; hence, worry, whether of body or mind." The word for "spoiling" means "violence; ravage or devastate." It is given in the King James Version as "desolation, destruction, oppression, robbery, spoil, and wasting."

The word for "violence" in Habakkuk 1:3 is the same as that used in verse 2 as well as Habakkuk 1:9; 2:8,17.

The words "strife" and "contention" are legal terms that describe our court system. "Strife" means "a contest (personal or legal); to toss, grapple; to wrangle, hold a controversy; defend." "Contention" means "a contest or quarrel."

Domestically, there is wife and child abuse. On Wall Street, there is economic abuse. Corrupt judges and lawyers, ignorant of the content and intent of our Constitution, have shredded justice with the scissors of Jehoiakim. In the church world, ministers have abused the people, sexually and spiritually. Little wonder that the people in the pew can't get along. They learned the tricks of religious warfare from their leaders. It's every man for himself.

Habakkuk poured out his complaint to the Lord. Why does the Lord allow His man to behold this evil? Why doesn't He do something about it? Without law, there is anarchy. Men will do as they please. A society without restraints forces us to live in a very dangerous time.

Hab. 1:4, KJV:

*Therefore the law is slacked, and judgment doth never go forth: for the wicked doth compass about the righteous; therefore wrong judgment proceedeth.*

Hab. 1:4, NIV:

*Therefore the law is paralyzed, and justice never prevails. The wicked hem in the righteous, so that justice is perverted.*

Hab. 1:4, TLB:

*The law is not enforced, and there is no justice given in the courts, for the wicked far outnumber the righteous, and bribes and trickery prevail.*

The word for "slacked" here means "to be sluggish," and is translated as "cease, be feeble, faint, be slacked." It could read, "The law is crippled," literally "paralyzed," nothing but a dead letter (2 Cor. 3:1-6). This has happened in America to two great documents: the Bible and the Constitution. Our nation was founded upon the Constitution, a document based upon the Word of God. We have abandoned it all to secular humanism. God's Law is the constitution for all men, the heart and soul of political, religious, and social life. The neglect of the Bible inevitably brings ruination to the land and its people.

Deut. 28:15, KJV:

*But it shall come to pass, if thou wilt not hearken unto the voice of the Lord thy God, to observe to do all His commandments and His statutes which I command thee this day; that all these curses shall come upon thee, and overtake thee.*

The word for "compass about" in Habakkuk 1:4 means "to enclose; in a hostile sense, to besiege." America is under siege from within and without. Like Habakkuk, we are living in a hostile environment. Our streets are not safe. We feel enclosed, trapped, with no real solution to our condition. The righteous people remaining in the land feel hedged in, restrained by the wicked so as to nullify any effort to re-establish the authority of God's Law. Consequently, judges will invariably favor the "right people"—their own cliques.

Where is God in all this? From hamlet to metroplex, there is a church on every corner, but where is the Word of the Lord? Why must the righteous suffer while the wicked flourish (Jer. 12:1-4; 15:15-18)?

On a personal level, things have happened to all of us for which there is no human answer. I've sat and held the hands of a lot of people in 25 years of ministry, and the worst feeling that a pastor has is not to have an answer for those who are hurting. "Why did it happen, preacher? How long do I have to stay under this burden?" We can only speak what we hear the Father say.

"Why, Lord?" we ask. "Because, My son, because..."

"How long, Lord?" we wonder. "It's up to you, My son, it's up to you..."

God will hear our cry. He is faithful. He is about to answer. He knows all about the problem. But like Habakkuk, we will be shocked at His reply.

## Chapter Four

# The Perplexity

### "Lo, I raise up the Chaldeans"

### Habakkuk 1:5-17

The opening verses of Habakkuk's prophecy revealed His *problem.* Having seen the injustice and unrighteousness that marked his day, the man of God had cried out, "How long?" and "Why?"

This kind of cry comes from the lower realms. It is void of vision and is not based on an understanding of the ways of the Lord. The heart of the prophet sobbed, surrounded and overwhelmed by circumstances, that is, the appearance of things. We hear the cry of a man who is walking by sight and not by faith, but it is a cry that God will answer.

Habakkuk's objections were based on what he saw with his natural eyes...sense knowledge, empirical knowledge, scientific and logical. What men see might be the facts, but not the truth. Unless it agrees with God, His Word and His nature, it is passing away...dying. It's not even real.

The prophet complained to the Lord. It's all right to complain as long as we take our complaint to the Lord. His ear is bent toward you concerning your life, your world, your country. He will tell you what He is about to do.

Hab. 1:5, KJV:

> *Behold ye among the heathen, and regard, and wonder marvellously: for I will work a work in your days, which ye will not believe, though it be told you.*

Hab. 1:5, TLB:

> *The Lord replied: "Look, and be amazed! You will be astounded at what I am about to do! For I am going to do something in your own lifetime that you will have to see to believe."*

The apostle Paul used these same words on his first missionary journey to proclaim the finished work of Jesus Christ, especially His resurrection from the dead (Acts 13:33-37).

Acts 13:40-41, KJV:

> *Beware therefore, lest that come upon you, which is spoken of in the prophets;*
> *Behold, ye despisers, and wonder, and perish: for I work a work in your days, a work which ye shall in no wise believe, though a man declare it unto you.*

Habakkuk got his answer, but it was not what he expected. He would "wonder marvellously," literally "be in consternation; be shocked, shudder." The prophet was amazed and astonished at the revelation of God's ways (1 Sam. 3:11).

"I will work a work" is literally "one is working a work" (see Ps. 64:9; 77:13; 90:16; 111:3). Behind the scenes, in the unseen realm of the Spirit, things are happening. Get ready, America! God is going to do something in our lifetime, in our generation, that we will have to see to believe. That which He is about to do in the earth is now being "told" by His servants the prophets.

Amos 3:7, KJV:

*Surely the Lord God will do nothing, but he revealeth His secret unto His servants the prophets.*

The word for "told" in Habakkuk 1:5 means "to score with a mark as a tally or record; to inscribe; intensively, to recount or celebrate." God desires to write His Word on the tables of every man's heart. His ways and His thoughts are always higher than ours. He is always able to go beyond what we are able to ask or think (Is. 55:8-9; Mt. 19:26; Eph. 3:20).

When men try to solve a spiritual problem with a natural solution, they soon learn that the remedy God gives brings even further *perplexity* than their original question.

When we ask, "How long?" and "Why?" with our brain instead of our heart, the answer from God is a shocker. Jehovah knew about the sins of Judah. He had warned them for over 100 years not to follow the example of the northern kingdom of Israel. At that time, Assyria was the rod of His anger. Now He would use another instrument...the Chaldeans!

The Babylonian army is described in Habakkuk 1:6-11 (from the Amplified Bible):

> *For behold! I am rousing up the Chaldeans, that bitter and impetuous nation, who march through the breadth of the earth, to take possession of dwelling places that do not belong to them. [II Kings 24:2.] [The Chaldeans] are terrible and dreadful; their justice and dignity proceed only from themselves. Their horses also are swifter than leopards and are more fierce than the evening wolves, and their horsemen spread themselves and press on proudly; yes, their horsemen come from afar; they fly like an eagle that hastens to devour. They all come for violence; their faces turn eagerly forward, and they gather prisoners together like sand. They scoff at kings, and rulers are a derision to them; they ridicule every stronghold, for they heap up dust [for earth mounds] and take it. Then they sweep by like a wind and pass on, and they load themselves with guilt, [as do all men] whose own power is their god.*

Habakkuk's *problem* has now become his *perplexity*. Jehovah had said, "The answer that I am bringing is ruthless, relentless, and invincible. It's coming, and you can't stop it." Are we willing to receive God the way He is coming to us? The early Church experienced great persecution but reached their generation with the gospel. God won't let America and the world go on and on. Something's got to give. We are surrounded by unrighteousness, but we're numb to it.

Like Judah, America has turned away from the Lord. In His sovereign wisdom and might, God now sends the

"Chaldeans" to correct us. They are now called the economy, immorality, and violence. In Chapter Two we looked at dozens of contemporary examples. Now let us examine the words of the prophet more closely. We are about to discover that he was also speaking to the plight of America.

### The Chaldeans Are Coming!

Hab. 1:6, KJV:

*For, lo, I raise up the Chaldeans, that bitter and hasty nation, which shall march through the breadth of the land, to possess the dwellingplaces that are not theirs.*

Hab. 1:6, TLB:

*I am raising a new force on the world scene, the Chaldeans, a cruel and violent nation who will march across the world and conquer it.*

A new force...a new world order...a new age...there is more than one cruel and violent nation on this planet. The word for "bitter" means "fierce, pitilessly cruel, bitter as poison." The word for "hasty" in this verse means "to hurry (in a bad sense)." Men today are running to do evil, swift to shed blood. The apostle describes our society in his letter to the Romans.

Rom. 3:14-18, KJV:

*Whose mouth is full of cursing and bitterness:*
*Their feet are swift to shed blood:*
*Destruction and misery are in their ways:*

*And the way of peace have they not known:*
*There is no fear of God before their eyes.*

Hab. 1:7, KJV:

*They are terrible and dreadful: their judgment and their dignity shall proceed of themselves.*

Hab. 1:7, TLB:

*They are notorious for their cruelty. They do as they like, and no one can interfere.*

Hab. 1:7, Ferrar Fenton:

*And with them are terror and fear; they make laws and rules for themselves.*

The Chaldeans are literally "frightful" and "to be feared." The word for "dignity" here can mean "an elevation" or "a leprous scab." Leprosy, like the sin of self-assumed superiority, numbs the senses.

The goals that men now seek after are dominated by the lusts of the flesh, the lust of the eyes, and the pride of life. No expense is spared in this pursuit of death. It doesn't matter if others are hurt along the way. Humanism and hedonism mark the minds and bodies of our youth on college campuses, and no one dare interfere. There is a new tongue among our children that we do not understand. Like the Babylonians of old, men today are "hasty," hurrying themselves onward, impetuously rushing on, never resting until their goal—the satisfaction of their flesh—is reached.

Deut. 28:49, KJV:

*The Lord shall bring a nation against thee from far, from the end of the earth, as swift as the eagle flieth; a nation whose tongue thou shalt not understand.*

We have here the warning of Moses. The purpose of the invaders is to perpetuate violence in the land. This was Judah's sin (Hab. 1:2-3), and it will be her punishment. Take heed, young person. What goes around comes around.

Hab. 1:8, KJV:

*Their horses also are swifter than the leopards, and are more fierce than the evening wolves: and their horsemen shall spread themselves, and their horsemen shall come from far; they shall fly as the eagle that hasteth to eat.*

Hab. 1:8, TLB:

*Their horses are swifter than leopards. They are a fierce people, more fierce than wolves at dusk. Their cavalry move proudly forward from a distant land; like eagles they come swooping down to pounce upon their prey.*

Hab. 1:9, KJV:

*They shall come all for violence: their faces shall sup up as the east wind, and they shall gather the captivity as the sand.*

Hab. 1:9, NIV:

*They all come bent on violence. Their hordes advance like a desert wind and gather prisoners like sand.*

Mt. 7:15, KJV:

> *Beware of false prophets, which come to you in sheep's clothing, but inwardly they are ravening wolves.*

Acts 20:29, KJV:

> *For I know this, that after my departing shall grievous wolves enter in among you, not sparing the flock.*

Their horses are "swifter" or "lighter" (light of foot) to spring down upon the prey. These are evening wolves, rapacious, mischievous, and injurious. They roam throughout the strata of society, then and now (Jer. 5:6; Zeph. 3:3). These false prophets and false words prey upon the innocent. These judges do not spare, being without mercy. Evening wolves graphically picture the youth gangs in our cities, who, after spending the day in their dens, gather at evening for their murderous raids.

The word for "sup" in Habakkuk 1:9 means "to swallow or gulp." It's supper time and the average American is on the menu. Our paychecks are being swallowed by increasing taxation. Verse 9 also speaks of the "east wind." This was the wind of the wilderness and was most violent. It was scorching, blackening, and blasting, sucking up all moisture and freshness. In Acts 27, the ship bound for Rome was destroyed by a tempestuous east wind called Euroclydon. So today there is a world system headed for the rocks. Thank God there is an apostolic man on board America's ship who has heard from God! When all hope has been dismissed, after we've tasted of darkness so dark we can feel it, this nation will be ready to listen to the Word of the Lord (Ex. 10:21-23; Acts 27:20-25).

The economy, immorality, and violence now "spread" themselves; they "act proudly or prance." Impulsive, insane new policies have swept down upon the American people. We are held captive in the land of the free. The word for "captivity" in verse 9 means "exiled." One of the English renderings means "to take away." The Chaldeans aren't coming. They are here, sent to strip us of our constitutional rights. It is amazing what self-serving lobbyists have plundered in the past 30 years.

2 Cor. 4:8, KJV:

*We are troubled on every side, yet not distressed; we are perplexed, but not in despair.*

The Greek word for "perplexed" here means "to have no way out; to be at a loss (mentally)." From the young man or woman in the ghetto to the elderly on a fixed income, there seems to be no answer, no way out. We spend billions on program after program, but the Chaldeans keep on coming. What a dilemma! What perplexity! Can a loving, caring, and supposedly sovereign God be sending all this stuff down on our heads?

When God's nation walked away from His Word in the Old Testament, He promised to correct them. Jeremiah, Habakkuk's prophetic peer, said that Nebuchadnezzar would come down like the eagle upon his foes (Jer. 48:40; Lam. 4:19). America is no different. God is no respecter of persons. His judgments now impact every level of our daily lives.

Deut. 28:49-50, NIV:

*The Lord will bring a nation against you from far away, from the ends of the earth, like an eagle swooping down, a nation whose language you will not understand,*

*a fierce-looking nation without respect for the old or pity for the young.*

Our senior citizens are coming under the rod of the economy, immorality, and violence. Having retired, they can't even walk or jog the streets of their neighborhoods. We used to carry books to school, not knives and guns. It all seems so unreal, but it is happening to all of us. Is there no end to this unrelenting swarm of evil?

Hab. 1:10, KJV:

*And they shall scoff at the kings, and the princes shall be a scorn unto them: they shall deride every strong hold; for they shall heap dust, and take it.*

Hab. 1:10, NIV:

*They deride kings and scoff at rulers. They laugh at all fortified cities; they build earthen ramps and capture them.*

Hab. 1:10, Ferrar Fenton:

*...they jeer at all fortifications.*

Hab. 1:11, KJV:

*Then shall his mind change, and he shall pass over, and offend, imputing this his power unto his god.*

Hab. 1:11, NIV:

*Then they sweep past like the wind and go on—guilty men, whose own strength is their god.*

Hab. 1:11, TLB:

*They sweep past like wind and are gone, but their guilt is deep, for they claim their power is from their gods.*

The words for "they" and "them" in verse 10 are literally "he" and "him," referring to the king of Babylon. Like most politicians and some preachers, Nebuchadnezzar was proud and arrogant. He "ridiculed" kings and made a "laughing-stock" of rulers (2 Kings 24–25; 2 Chron. 36). He mocked and despised any kind of government but his own. The word for "deride" in verse 10 means "to laugh; to play." It's just a game to the king of confusion. It seems that no one can stand before him. He is invincible, "taking" every stronghold and fortress, for his foes have been "caught in a net, trap, or pit."

One notable thing about Chaldeans, past and present: They claim their power is from their gods (Dan. 4:30; 2 Thess. 2:3-4). The prophet Isaiah addressed the Babylonians about their idolatry.

Is. 47:13, KJV:

*Thou art wearied in the multitude of thy counsels. Let now the astrologers, the stargazers, the monthly prognosticators, stand up, and save thee from these things that shall come upon thee.*

Is. 47:13, NIV:

*All the counsel you have received has only worn you out! Let your astrologers come forward, those stargazers who make predictions month by month, let them save you from what is coming upon you.*

Babylonian religion was temple-centered, with elaborate festivals and many different types of priests, especially exorcists and diviners. The Bible's contempt for astrology is most clearly seen in its prohibition of any technique to aid in predicting the future. Astrology assumes that God does not control history. It assumes that history is governed by the affairs of the pagan gods as revealed in the movement of the planets. True believers know that a sovereign God rules this world and that resorting to astrology is a denial of the life of faith by which one trusts God, not his lucky stars, for the future.

Psychic hotlines are big business, especially those peddled by famous worldly personalities. Dealing with familiar spirits is banned in the Bible, yet practiced by the leaders of our government. The size of this volume will not permit us to deal with the occult. Suffice it to say that it was a way of life to the Babylonians and is on the rise in America. Then and now, such practitioners are heathen, eating daily at the table of devils. We are being blitzed by 900 numbers and strange voices. Beware, friend. That mess will wear you out. Moreover, it won't save you from what's coming.

1 Cor. 10:21, KJV:

*Ye cannot drink the cup of the Lord, and the cup of devils: ye cannot be partakers of the Lord's table, and of the table of devils.*

1 Cor. 10:21, NIV:

*You cannot drink the cup of the Lord and the cup of demons too; you cannot have a part in both the Lord's table and the table of demons.*

Certainly Judah had sinned. But the Chaldeans were by far more wicked. No wonder Habakkuk was perplexed. None of this made sense. Perhaps he could convince the Lord to do otherwise. Hear his plea.

### This Is Not the Answer We Expected

Hab. 1:12, KJV:

*Art Thou not from everlasting, O Lord my God, mine Holy One? we shall not die. O Lord, Thou hast ordained them for judgment; and, O mighty God, Thou hast established them for correction.*

Hab. 1:12, TLB:

*O Lord my God, my Holy One, You who are eternal— is Your plan in all of this to wipe us out? Surely not! O God our Rock, You have decreed the rise of these Chaldeans to chasten and correct us for our awful sins.*

Hab. 1:13, KJV:

*Thou art of purer eyes than to behold evil, and canst not look on iniquity: wherefore lookest Thou upon them that deal treacherously, and holdest Thy tongue when the wicked devoureth the man that is more righteous than he?*

Hab. 1:13, TLB:

*We are wicked, but they far more! Will You, who cannot allow sin in any form, stand idly by while they swallow us up? Should You be silent while the wicked destroy those who are better than they?*

Hab. 1:13, Ferrar Fenton:

*Your pure eyes never sanction the wrong, and oppression You will not endure; then why do You look on the traitors, and are dumb when the bad rob the good?*

Habakkuk was shocked! Surely God would not judge Judah in such a way. After all, the patriarch Abraham was called out of the same idolatry, out of Ur of the Chaldees (Gen. 12:1-3). Many of us never thought we would live to see the things that have come upon our nation. These Chaldeans had been "ordained" or "set" by the Lord. Jehovah had established them for "correction." This meant that Babylon was now God's instrument sent to "argue against, convict, dispute, judge, reprove, and rebuke" Judah.

Habakkuk addressed God in verse 12 as the "mighty God," literally, "Rock." This was a title much used by David in the Psalms. God was Judah's might and Upholder, the sole Source of all strength, the Supporter of all which is upheld. The stability of Habakkuk's world, all that he knew or understood about Jehovah, was falling apart.

What seeming injustice! The prophet's head was reeling. He knew that the Chaldeans were evil and idolatrous. Why would the Lord even look at those who dealt so "treacherously?" This word in verse 13 means "to cover (with a garment); to act covertly; to pillage." It is translated in the King James Version as "deal deceitfully, unfaithfully; to offend or transgress."

The Chaldeans were seasoned politickers. Their interests were totally self-serving. Like most marriages today, relationships were more business-oriented, and were only entered into for one's own benefit and gain. "What's in it for me?" is the Chaldean calling card, not "What can I give?" Sadder still are the multitudes of God's people who go to the church of their choice, lusting after the blessings but ignoring God's covenantal requirements.

Hab. 1:14, KJV:

> *And makest men as the fishes of the sea, as the creeping things, that have no ruler over them?*

Hab. 1:14, TLB:

> *Are we but fish, to be caught and killed? Are we but creeping things that have no leader to defend them from their foes?*

Hab. 1:15, KJV:

> *They take up all of them with the angle, they catch them in their net, and gather them in their drag: therefore they rejoice and are glad.*

Hab. 1:15, TLB:

> *Must we be strung up on their hooks and dragged out in their nets, while they rejoice?*

The nations were the sea, men were the fish, and Nebuchadnezzar of Babylon was the fisherman. They have "no ruler," no government by which to defend themselves against anyone. We have taken the Bible out of our schools and churches. We have butchered the Constitution. There is no "ruler," no canon, no standard of measurement, no clear definition of right and wrong.

Judg. 21:25, KJV:

> *In those days there was no king in Israel: every man did that which was right in his own eyes.*

The word for "angle" in verse 15 means "a hook." The word for "drag" means "a fisher's net." Some feel that the "angle" was a smaller net cast by hand and the "drag" a larger one weighted to sink to the bottom and dragged to the boat or the shore. When relationships are begun for political reasons, there's always an angle, a hook. The string is attached, and now it's choking the average American to death, especially those at the bottom of society. The lower and middle classes are being raked, caught, and swept away in a net weighted by insensitive bureaucracy.

Hab. 1:16, KJV:

> *Therefore they sacrifice unto their net, and burn incense unto their drag; because by them their portion is fat, and their meat plenteous.*

Hab. 1:16, TLB:

> *Then they will worship their nets and burn incense before them! "These are the gods who make us rich," they'll say.*

Hab. 1:17, KJV:

> *Shall they therefore empty their net, and not spare continually to slay the nations?*

Hab. 1:17, NIV:

*Is he to keep on emptying his net, destroying nations without mercy?*

Even more perplexing is that the Chaldeans worship the cruelty and injustice by which they rule. Will no one intervene? When will this madness cease? The foundations of the earth are out of course. What is the righteous man to do (Ps. 11:3)?

The word for "slay" in verse 17 means "to smite with deadly intent, to murder." Like the typical Hollywood summer movie full of senseless killing and violence, the Chaldeans are relentless and ruthless. Shall these cruel wolves and leopards keep on emptying their net after having made another rich catch—shall the rich keep getting richer? Are we to envy the rich and the famous as they amass works of art, silver and gold, power and glory? None of this makes sense to the prophet. His own wisdom and strength is no match for the answer of the Lord.

Many of God's people are dismayed, even frightened. Traditional evangelical and pentecostal teachings and methods cannot keep pace with the pressures of this decade. False prophets have come and gone who said we'd never see the 90s!

We must hear from the Lord. Our sobbing and musings have brought a response from Him, but these days are different, to say the least. No one can read the handwriting on the wall; everyone is too busy banging his head against it!

That's our problem...our heads...our reason. That's why we cannot rest in the day of trouble. In my book, *The More Excellent Ministry*, I gave a detailed study in Chapter Seven showing that the mark of the beast is a present reality (Rev. 13:13-18). That mark or character (nature) was in the forehead and the right hand. All human wisdom and all human strength, apart from the Holy Ghost, is beastly. Head-and-shoulders men, whether in corporate America or denominational headquarters, are running scared. We didn't expect this kind of tribulation. The Chaldeans are here and we don't know what to do.

The prophet was not happy about the way God was taking care of the problem. After having failed to impress the Lord by logic and human argument, Habakkuk finally sensed that it was time to listen, not to speak. He had pleaded with the Lord, but Jehovah was not in a plea-bargaining mood. The man of God had sobbed until there was no more strength to sob; so he now retires to the only place where anything makes sense: the place of transcendent prayer.

# PART TWO:
# THE VISION

## Seeing Faith

# Chapter Five

# The Prayer

**"The vision is yet for an appointed time"**

**Habakkuk 2:1-4**

Hab. 2:1, KJV:

*I will stand upon my watch, and set me upon the tower, and will watch to see what He will say unto me, and what I shall answer when I am reproved.*

Hab. 2:1, TLB:

*I will climb my watchtower now and wait to see what answer God will give to my complaint.*

Mk. 13:33, KJV:

*Take ye heed, watch and pray: for ye know not when the time is.*

Eph. 6:13-14, KJV:

*Wherefore take unto you the whole armour of God, that ye may be able to withstand in the evil day, and having done all, to stand.*

*Stand therefore, having your loins girt about with truth, and having on the breastplate of righteousness.*

Habakkuk had been bold, daring to contend, to argue, to remonstrate with God. The prophet was distressed at the inscrutable dealings of Jehovah with His people. Habakkuk had complained at first of the widespread iniquity in Judah. Once he had learned of the rod of God's anger, he had bowed down in greater mental agony that God should use the Chaldeans, a nation even less righteous than his own. Since God had answered his first questionings, he was confident that Jehovah would do likewise with his greater problem. Thus he assumed the heart attitude of a watchman.

Habakkuk was a seer. His vision took place in the realm of the Spirit. Futility and frustration come when men attempt to solve spiritual problems with natural answers, with their brains and not their hearts. America's problems are spiritual problems that require spiritual solutions. We must see things from God's point of view, from the perspective of the heavens, not the earth (Song 4:8; Phil. 3:20). There was no vision until the prophet moved to the higher level, transcending his present circumstances.

Far from solving Habakkuk's *problem*, the Lord's revelation of His impending judgment upon Judah had raised only new questions, new doubts, new fears. Yet the prophet did not permit this *perplexity* to turn him away in unbelief from the Lord, even though God's ways seemed incomprehensible at the time. He would approach the Lord a third time in *prayer* with the hope of finally receiving a satisfying answer.

"I will stand upon *my* watch...." No one else's watch. This is the place of personal prayer. Habakkuk had to pray in his day for his nation, and we in ours for America. Christian friend, we are responsible for our generation. Do you have a watch, and what are you watching for? Change channels...watch with the eyes of your heart, not the eyes of your head.

Mk. 6:48, KJV:

*And He saw them toiling in rowing; for the wind was contrary unto them: and about the fourth watch of the night He cometh unto them, walking upon the sea, and would have passed by them.*

The New International Version says that the disciples were "straining at the oars." In America today, the Wind of the Holy Spirit is contrary to all the ways of the flesh (Gal. 5:17). The "fourth watch" was about 3 a.m., the darkest hour. We've rowed all night. The beast system has worn us out (Dan. 7:25). Take heart, friends. God is about to show up and get in our boat! He alone can take us to the "other side."

God is calling this nation to prayer. Jesus Christ is the only way to the Father (Jn. 14:6). As the Door (Jn. 10:9), He is the only valid entry into this dimension of the supernatural. In His name, we can talk to God and make our petitions known. The phrase "unto me" in Habakkuk 2:1 is literally "in me." Habakkuk would see what the Lord would say "in" him! Compare verse 20 of chapter two and remember that the Lord is closer than we think: He lives and speaks in the hearts of men!

The word for "stand" in verse 1 means "to place (any thing so as to stay); to station, offer, or continue." The prophet had a made-up mind. He "set" or planted himself firmly before the Lord in prayer and did not move until he heard from Heaven. Few are willing to offer themselves this way in intercession. Habakkuk was a lonely sentinel in the day of trouble. He continued in this posture of humility until the heavens opened. We must pray for our people and our nation. We must pray until we see the Lord.

2 Chron. 7:14, KJV:

> *If My people, which are called by My name, shall humble themselves, and pray, and seek My face, and turn from their wicked ways; then will I hear from heaven, and will forgive their sin, and will heal their land.*

The "tower" in Habakkuk 2:1 speaks of that which is strong, firm, and reliable (Prov. 18:10), a "fenced place." We can stand on the solid Rock, Christ Jesus, the Word of God (Jn. 1:1). Also, the Constitution of our great nation "towers" over the landmark decisions made in 1947, 1962, and 1973. We must return to the basic freedoms that our fathers died for. Let us call America back to its Christian roots. We must re-establish fences or limits—we used to call them values.

The word for "will watch" in Habakkuk 2:1 is most descriptive. It means "to lean forward, to peer into the distance; to observe, to await." Habakkuk was a "watchman." A watchtower was an observation tower upon which a guard or lookout was stationed to keep watch, an elevated structure offering an extensive view (2 Kings 17:9; 18:8; Is. 21:8). From that vantage point, the watchman would lift up his eyes. Habakkuk took his station in prayer like a servant awaiting the word of his master.

Here is the key to understanding this ancient prophecy and the answer to our present national situation. In the 90s, men must transcend a time-space world and enter the dimension of eternal spirit, the throne room of the living God! We must peer off into the distance until we, like our Heavenly Father, can see the end from the beginning. Until we receive a vision of the "bigger picture," we will worry ourselves to death over the economy, immorality, and violence. We must ascend the hill of the Lord. We must climb Jacob's ladder. We must rise above the sob of an order that is passing away. We must wait upon the Lord until we are "reproved," literally, "chastised or corrected." This word comes from a root which means "to be right." Everybody can't be right. Who's right? *He* is! Who shall stand when He appears? *He* will!

## Tell It Like It Is

Hab. 2:2, KJV:

*And the Lord answered me, and said, Write the vision, and make it plain upon tables, that he may run that readeth it.*

Hab. 2:2, NIV:

*Then the Lord replied: "Write down the revelation and make it plain on tablets so that a herald may run with it."*

Hab. 2:2, TLB:

*And the Lord said to me, "Write My answer on a billboard, large and clear, so that anyone can read it at a glance and rush to tell the others."*

What comfort! What relief! When we call, the Lord will answer! He wants to "write" His words upon our hearts. This word means "to describe, inscribe, prescribe, and subscribe." We are to be His letter, His epistle, until all men subscribe to His voice (2 Cor. 5:17-21).

The Lord commanded Habakkuk to write the revelation upon tablets (Is. 8:1; Jer. 17:1). They could have been like those in the marketplace upon which public notices were written, graven in clay in large, clear letters. These tablets were erected in public places, on highways, perhaps in the temple courts...wherever they would attract the attention of the people hurrying by on their way to work, to business, to worship, to play, to sin.

The word for "vision" in verse 2 means "a sight, dream, revelation, or oracle." The root is "to gaze at; to perceive or contemplate (with pleasure)." Is your dream His dream? Your vision His vision? Your pleasure His pleasure? Your will His will? The American people and the American Church have set their sights on other things.

To every pastor and leader comes this gnawing question: "Have you stayed true to the original vision?" Or have other voices seduced you away from the simplicity, the singleness, that is in Christ? Every leader in our nation's capital must search his heart: "Have I stayed true to the original vision, the Declaration of Independence and the Constitution, by which the founding fathers framed a Christian nation?"

Deut. 27:8, KJV:

*And thou shalt write upon the stones all the words of this law very plainly.*

1 Pet. 2:5, KJV:

*Ye also, as lively stones, are built up a spiritual house, an holy priesthood, to offer up spiritual sacrifices, acceptable to God by Jesus Christ.*

2 Cor 3:3, TLB:

*They can see that you are a letter from Christ, written by us. It is not a letter written with pen and ink, but by the Spirit of the living God; not one carved on stone, but in human hearts.*

Our only hope is that somebody watches and prays until God's purpose is made "plain." This word means "to dig, to engrave; figuratively, to explain." There is an answer, an explanation, but it only makes sense when God explains it—on His turf and in His time. He is writing it in large, clear "upper-case" (Eph. 2:6) letters as He plows with an apostolic Word that has begun to "dig" into this generation. Then we can live "plain" and be easy to "read."

The final phrase in Habakkuk 2:1, "that he may run that readeth it," pictures a generation on the run. Americans are the most mobile people in the earth, always moving. With more modern conveniences and less time, we are never satisfied and can't keep still. We and our children (thanks to our humanistic educational system) have stopped reading, writing, and meditating. Never having enough time to do all our running around, we only glance at things. We are 28 miles wide and a quarter-inch deep.

The prophet was instructed that his vision was to be written upon "tables," literally, upon "polished tablets of stone, wood, or metal." God is dealing with this nation. He wants to write His law upon the tables of our hearts. America has lost its heart. God is looking for something to write on. Turn to Him in this day of fresh vision and hope.

### Jesus Is the Answer

Hab. 2:3, KJV:

*For the vision is yet for an appointed time, but at the end it shall speak, and not lie: though it tarry, wait for it; because it will surely come, it will not tarry.*

Hab. 2:3, NIV:

*For the revelation awaits an appointed time; it speaks of the end and will not prove false. Though it linger, wait for it; it will certainly come and will not delay.*

Hab. 2:3, TLB:

*But these things I plan won't happen right away. Slowly, steadily, surely, the time approaches when the vision will be fulfilled. If it seems slow, do not despair, for these things will surely come to pass. Just be patient! They will not be overdue a single day!*

Five things are said of the "vision" that Habakkuk saw:

1. *It was yet for an appointed time.*
2. *It would speak at the end.*
3. *It would not lie.*
4. *It would tarry.*
5. *It would surely come.*

The writer to the Hebrews quotes this verse. Moving from the Old to the New Testament, we discover that the "vision" is a Person! Habakkuk saw the Lord! His sob became a song because he saw Jesus.

Heb. 10:37, KJV:

*For yet a little while, and **He** that shall come will come, and will not tarry.*

We must understand this truth about the vision: *"It"* becomes *"He"*!

The vision moves from the abstract to the real, from the type to the antitype, from the shadow to the substance. Men in the world and men in the Church have all put their eggs in one basket: whatever their understanding of "it" is. Everyone is waiting in his own way for "it" to happen. The nation waits for some new presidential policy package; maybe "it" will work...the Church for some new eschatological view; maybe "it" will be the right one. We must be delivered from this futility. "It" was not the answer for Judah and is not the answer for America. "He" is the Answer, and His name is Jesus! While men wait for "it" to happen, or for Bill Clinton to do "it," "He" is here (Gal. 4:6; Heb. 1:1-3)! The five things that Habakkuk said about the vision ("it") are true of "Him."

1. *He was yet for an appointed time.*
2. *He would speak at the end.*
3. *He would not lie.*
4. *He would tarry.*
5. *He would surely come.*

First, Jesus Christ was yet for an "appointed time." This word means "an appointment, a fixed time or season, a festival." This term makes direct reference to the Old Testament Feasts of the Lord: Passover, Pentecost, and Tabernacles.

Deut. 16:16, KJV:

*Three times in a year shall all thy males appear before the Lord thy God in the place which He shall choose; in the feast of unleavened bread, and in the feast of weeks, and in the feast of tabernacles: and they shall not appear before the Lord empty.*

Habakkuk saw something greater than Judah, more powerful than the Chaldeans, bigger than America's problems. Habakkuk saw Jesus, the Word made flesh (Jn. 1:14). What he saw became a song (chapter 3) about the Lord and His ultimate victory over all His enemies. In the Feast of Passover, Jesus is Savior (Jn. 1:29). In the Feast of Pentecost, He baptizes men with the Holy Ghost, just as He did in the Book of Acts (Mt. 3:11). In the Feast of Tabernacles, He is King and Lord, harvesting the nations, filling the earth with His glory (Rev. 19:16; 21:3-4). Habakkuk's "vision" revealed these three feasts, each to be fulfilled in Jesus Christ and His Church.

Secondly, Jesus Christ would "speak" at the "end." Jesus is the Word (Jn. 1:1; Heb. 1:1). He is the sum total of all that God has spoken to man. The only hope for America and the world is the One who tabernacles among us (Jn. 1:14-18). He is the first and last Word on the subject. He is the Alpha and the Omega, the Beginning and the End. When He died on the cross, He brought an "end" to the Old Covenant, and ushered in a new and living way through His shed blood. He ended the world of the law, ushering in grace and truth (Jn. 19:30; Heb. 9:26).

The word for "end" in Habakkuk 2:3 means "an extremity." Jesus Christ paid the supreme sacrifice and is now able to save us to the uttermost (Heb. 7:25). Some may feel stretched to the max, but the Lord can minister to any situation, no matter how extreme the circumstances.

The word for "speak" means "to puff, to blow with the breath; to fan (as a breeze), to kindle (a fire)." Compare the Greek word for "spirit" (*pněuma*) which means "spirit, wind, or breath." Jesus came from the Father and went to the Father, who then sent the Holy Spirit to speak to our hearts, to reveal the Son, to guide us into the vision and plan of the Creator for His whole creation (Song 4:16; Jn. 16:13).

The vision that Habakkuk saw literally "pants" or "gasps" on to its fulfillment. It seeks the accomplishment of the things it predicts. As the runner who sees the goal coming nearer strains every muscle and runs the faster, until his breath comes in loud gasps, so the vision sees the end of the race. Ultimately, this is the "gasp" of Romans 8:19, the groan of all men and nations.

Rom. 8:19, KJV:

*For the earnest expectation of the creature waiteth for the manifestation of the sons of God.*

Rom. 8:19, NIV:

*The creation waits in eager expectation for the sons of God to be revealed.*

The promised Messiah was to be the Firstborn among many brethren (Rom. 8:29). The vision will not disappoint, but will surely come to pass. The Concordant Version of the Old Testament reads, "And it will bud at the end." Jesus Christ, the promised Seed of the woman (Gen. 3:15), would come and be planted in the earth. He would be the True Vine, the Resurrection and the Life (Jn. 11:25; 15:1-5).

Thirdly, Jesus Christ would not "lie." This word means "to deceive." The political world and the church world is full of deception. Men will lie to you. Jesus will not lie, because Jesus cannot lie. He tells the truth because He *is* the Truth (Jn. 14:6). His Spirit, the Spirit of the Son, the Spirit of Truth, has been sent into our hearts (Gal. 4:6). Interestingly, the Concordant Version of the Old Testament renders that as the vision "will not lie dormant." That is certainly true of Jesus. It was impossible for death to hold Him (Acts 2:24)!

Fourthly, Jesus Christ, the focal point of Habakkuk's vision, would "tarry." He would come in the proper time and season.

Gal. 4:4, KJV:

*But when the fulness of the time was come, God sent forth His Son, made of a woman, made under the law.*

Gal. 4:4, TLB:

> *But when the right time came, the time God decided on, He sent His Son, born of a woman, born as a Jew.*

Remember that Habakkuk saw this vision over 600 years before Jesus was born! This vision would "tarry" for over six centuries. God is never late. He is always on time—His time. Things look bleak in our nation, but God is on the way. Though the great revival He will bring seems to tarry, we must wait for it. The stage is now being set as God begins to intervene in the affairs of the nations.

We must "wait" upon the Lord (Ps. 33:20; Zeph. 3:8). This word comes from a root which means "to entrench." We must dig in and stay put before the Lord. He Himself is the Surety and the Guarantee of the New Covenant. He will do what He said He would do.

Lastly, Jesus Christ would "surely" come. In this sense, He will not "tarry," literally, "loiter, be behind, or procrastinate." God's purpose is sure. His Word and will are sure. In Him is no variableness or shadow of turning (Jas. 1:17). He has set His hand in motion. All the nations shall see and know that He is the Lord.

Is. 40:5, KJV:

> *And the glory of the Lord shall be revealed, and all flesh shall see it together: for the mouth of the Lord hath spoken it.*

At Habakkuk's time, the believers had waited, hoped, and prayed for more than 33 centuries for the Messiah (Gen. 3:15). Still God tells the prophet, "The vision is yet for an appointed time." Not because God had forgotten His promise or was no longer willing to perform it, but because He was still Jehovah, the eternal, almighty God. Only His appointed time had not yet arrived.

The vision is for an appointed time, but we want it now. Are you satisfied with your life? Have you and your local church completely fulfilled your mission? There is both an individual destiny and a corporate destiny. It takes God years to get some people into running position. Too many see the problems in America and say, "What's the use? Why bother? We can't help anyone."

Bill Clinton hasn't delivered on his "promises." The American Church is presently rethinking the false hope of the "any-minute rapture" theory. Reality is setting in. The only certainty these days is the faith of God Himself.

Whatever is troubling you, look until "it" becomes *Jesus*!

### The Just Shall Live by Faith

Hab. 2:4, KJV:

*Behold, his soul which is lifted up is not upright in him: but the just shall live by his faith.*

Hab. 2:4, NIV:

*See, he is puffed up; his desires are not upright—but the righteous will live by his faith.*

Hab. 2:4, NKJ:

*Behold the proud, his soul is not upright in him; but the just shall live by his faith.*

Hab. 2:4, TLB:

*Note this: Wicked men trust themselves alone [as these Chaldeans do], and fail; but the righteous man trusts in Me and lives!*

Hab. 2:4, Rotherham, The Emphasized Bible:

*Lo! As for the conceited one, crooked is his soul within him; but one who is righteous by his faithfulness shall live.*

This is the key verse to Habakkuk's entire prophecy. Because of its importance, let's review the three times in the New Testament it is quoted:

Rom. 1:17, KJV:

*For therein is the righteousness of God revealed from faith to faith: as it is written, The just shall live by faith.*

Gal. 3:11, KJV:

*But that no man is justified by the law in the sight of God, it is evident: for, The just shall live by faith.*

Heb. 10:38, KJV:

*Now the just shall live by faith: but if any man draw back, My soul shall have no pleasure in him.*

Habakkuk 2:4, though describing the arrogant Nebuchadnezzar and the humble prophet, shows the great contrast between the unbeliever and the Christian. The former is proud in heart, perverted in mind, and restless in soul. The latter confides in the Word, lives by his faith in the Word, and is delivered by the Word. There are two kinds of people in America: saints and ain'ts. This verse shows the difference between the believer and the unbeliever—two hearts, two natures, two orders—the new man and the old man, Christ and Adam, beauty and the beast.

The soul of the proud Babylonian is puffed up, full of deceit and dishonesty (Dan. 4). This way is the path to destruction. Men are proud and "lifted up," literally, "swelled, like a boil." This word is used in Deuteronomy 28:27 (translated as "emerods") to describe hemorrhoids, or piles, a fitting description of Chaldeans past and present. Certain groups are a pain to America. They are haughty and presumptuous. They are not "upright," or "straight." Interestingly, if one is gay, he is not "straight." Don't we have enough sense to know that if something is not straight, it is crooked or perverse?

When President Clinton inherited the Oval Office, he inherited an office of confusion. It will require more than the wisdom and strength of man to unravel this great human mess. It will require the faith and faithfulness of God. Our leaders will have to know the Heavenly Father through Jesus Christ, His Son. As a nation, we must repent; our sins must be washed away by His blood. We must exchange our filthy religious and political rags for the garments of His righteousness (Rev. 19:8).

Habakkuk saw what every man must see: "The righteous shall live by *His* [God's] faith." The word for "righteous" here means "just; to be right (in a moral sense)." America is sick because the whole creation is sick. It will take more than man's faith in God to heal our nation; it will take God's faith in Himself *in man*. It will take the faith of God.

This cannot be a hit-or-miss situation. We don't have time to experiment. We must hear from God. Both the Hebrew and Greek words for "faith" mean that which is "certain." The Hebrew *âman* (aw-man) is transliterated into the English "amen." So be it. The Greek *pistis* means "to rely by an inward certainty." What America needs now is something "certain,"—those rock-bottom values and spiritual absolutes upon which it was established. This kind of faith cannot be affected by the external, circumstantial appearance of the flesh realm. Habakkuk's vision is certain; it will surely come to pass!

In the third chapter of my book, *The More Excellent Ministry*, and the twelfth chapter of my book, *The Priesthood Is Changing*, I explained the meaning of going "from faith to faith" (Rom. 1:17). We must move out of the Old Covenant realm of faith (Heb. 11) and into the New Covenant realm of faith (Heb. 12:1-2). We must move out of basic, elementary faith into the faith authored by Jesus Christ, who was God in the flesh (1 Tim. 3:16). The "faith" churches of this nation have laid a good foundation, but now it is time to go on to maturity. The Bible, the Word of God, *is* the answer for America, but let's preach all of it! "First principles faith" alone will not move or heal this generation.

Heb. 6:1-2, KJV:

> *Therefore leaving the principles of the doctrine of Christ, let us go on unto perfection; not laying again*

*the foundation of repentance from dead works, and of faith toward God,*

*Of the doctrine of baptisms, and of laying on of hands, and of resurrection of the dead, and of eternal judgment.*

This foundational faith is faith "toward," literally "upon," God (1 Pet. 5:7). It is essentially man-centered and need-oriented. It reveals God's hand, what He can do for men in the name of Jesus. It is the "faith" message we have known for the last 20 years, and it is faith for:

1. *Regeneration (a new heart through a new birth)
   and justification (a new legal standing with God).*

Jn. 3:7, KJV:

*Marvel not that I said unto thee, Ye must be born again.*

2. *The circumcision of the heart in water baptism by immersion in the name of the Lord Jesus Christ.*

Col. 2:11-12, KJV:

*In whom also ye are circumcised with the circumcision made without hands, in putting off the body of the sins of the flesh by the circumcision of Christ:*

*Buried with Him in baptism, wherein also ye are risen with Him through the faith of the operation of God, who hath raised Him from the dead.*

3. *The Pentecostal experience of the Holy Ghost baptism with the initial evidence of speaking with other tongues.*

Acts 2:4, KJV:

*And they were all filled with the Holy Ghost, and began to speak with other tongues, as the Spirit gave them utterance.*

4. *The healing of man, physically and emotionally.*

1 Pet. 2:24, KJV:

*Who His own self bare our sins in His own body on the tree, that we, being dead to sins, should live unto righteousness: by whose stripes ye were healed.*

5. *The meeting of our personal financial needs.*

Phil. 4:19, KJV:

*But my God shall supply all your need according to His riches in glory by Christ Jesus.*

These personal New Covenant blessings are wonderful, but something greater than "elementary" faith will be needed to turn this nation back to God. Habakkuk's prayer and vision lifted his eyes to something greater than his own personal needs. God's purposes are generational; His plan worldwide. Its fullest outworked measure lies ahead, in the appointed time: the Feast of Tabernacles.

Don't waste your time in the lower realms. Seek those things which are above (Col. 3:1). Get on your watch. Station yourself until you see God. The vision is yet for the festival, not one day overdue.

Habakkuk had gone to the watchtower to hear and ended up seeing! With wonder, he looked off into the distance and beheld a time when the knowledge of the glory of the Lord would cover the earth as the waters cover the sea.

Lifted above his present dilemma, he bore witness to the faithfulness and justice of God in every aspect, even in Jehovah's predetermined destiny for King Nebuchadnezzar and his armies. Though they served as the rod of His anger, the Chaldeans would be judged. God was about to bring the hammer down in five swift strokes upon the head of Babylon's godless king.

## Chapter Six

# The Purging

*"A taunting proverb"*

**Habakkuk 2:5-20**

God must deal with every enemy of His Kingdom. We can rest with Habakkuk as we hear how Jehovah will judge and remove the Chaldeans, stripping them of their pride and might. Through the power of transcendent prayer, the prophet understood that the Creator interrupts the affairs of men.

Jehovah judged King Nebuchadnezzar and so He has begun a *purging* of America and the nations. God will intervene concerning the economy, immorality, and violence. Every nation in the earth will reel under the hammer of His hand. We are not going to carry our mess into His Kingdom. The Church will rise as the dust of true justice settles beneath His feet. The sword of the Lord comes down five times upon the Babylonian mindset, past and present, as outlined in Habakkuk 2:5-20.

*Introduction (2:5)*

1. *Woe to the ambitious and dishonest (2:6-8).*
2. *Woe to the proud and self-exalted (2:9-11).*
3. *Woe to the violent and shedders of blood (2:12-13).*

*Interlude (2:14)*

4. *Woe to the corrupt and debased (2:15-17).*
5. *Woe to the false worshipers and false gods (2:18-19).*

*Conclusion (2:20)*

The remainder of chapter 2 is a five-fold judgment upon Babylon. It is judgment upon the beast nature and the beast system. Habakkuk's five woes describe sin and the sinner in America. These plagues have eaten away our moral fiber until this nation has become rapacious, unscrupulous, sanguinary, intemperate, and idolatrous.

The Lord judged proud Babylon. He is coming now to deal with us, to purge His Church, corporately and individually. Before we examine these five specifics, we need to know who we are dealing with. It's easy to recognize a Chaldean. In fact, there's a little bit of Babylon in all of us.

### Seven Ways to Spot a Chaldean

Hab. 2:5, KJV:

*Yea also, because he transgresseth by wine, he is a proud man, neither keepeth at home, who enlargeth his desire as hell, and is as death, and cannot be satisfied, but gathereth unto him all nations, and heapeth unto him all people.*

Hab. 2:5, NIV:

*Indeed, wine betrays him; he is arrogant and never at rest. Because he is as greedy as the grave and like death is never satisfied, he gathers to himself all the nations and takes captive all the peoples.*

Hab. 2:5, TLB:

*What's more, these arrogant Chaldeans are betrayed by all their wine, for it is treacherous. In their greed they have collected many nations, but like death and hell, they are never satisfied.*

These five woes are taken up and uttered by all the nations and peoples who suffered at the hand of the cruel oppressor. So begins the taunting song to Babylonians everywhere, then and now:

**Who transgress by wine.** This word means to "cover with a garment, to act covertly; by implication, to pillage." The Hebrew literally reads, "Wine is a deceiver." The Concordant Version of the Old Testament says that "wine is treacherous."

Nebuchadnezzar is here represented in his usual character. Contemporary Chaldeans also love to drink. Sipping saints can be found in most churches. Drunkenness and debauchery is the common, anticipated weekend life style on every major college campus. Bacchus, the god of wine, is faithfully worshiped by the party animals. Alcohol is big business in America.

Those inebriated with their own successes live in towers they have built for themselves. Secret sins. Secret thoughts. Deals under the table...dirty, underhanded, political. Raping and pillaging others through relationships governed by the lord of darkness. But wine is treacherous. This is one hangover that won't go away.

**Who is a proud man.** This word means "elated or arrogant" (Prov. 21:24). Its root means "a mountain or a range of hills." Companies, religious systems, political entities loom high all around us, overwhelming the common man. But everything except the mountain of His Kingdom is coming down in the Day of the Lord. The wind is blowing from the north, coming to remove everything that God did not tell us to do. The wicked will not mock the righteous much longer. The proud are going to fall.

**Who does not keep at home.** This word means to "rest (as at home)." The idea here is that there is a beauty, celebration, and satisfaction that causes one to abide. Americans are the most restless people in the world, always on the go. Monogamy in marriage and covenant commitment in the local church have been exchanged for self-indulgent living motivated by the lust of the flesh. The thought that the greatest vocation for some women is to be a keeper at home, a lover of one husband and her children, appears outdated. Divorce in the home and covenant-breaking in the local church are rampant. What some call church growth in America is nothing more than fish changing tanks. The home is the basic unit of society. Every church problem is a home problem. As our homes go, so goes the church and the nation. What will it take to learn that again?

**Who enlarges his desire as hell.** A typical Chaldean stays busy by "broadening" his "desire," literally his "soul" (*nephesh*). Man's soul (*psuche* in the Greek) is his intellect, his emotions, and his will; that is, what he thinks, what he feels, what he wants. The last message that the average American Christian wants to hear is that he must lay down his "life" (*psuche*) for others. We are as "greedy as the grave." Every man is out to go for the gusto. Family life is shattered as we learn the bitter lesson that things do not satisfy. We are never at rest.

**Who is as death**. We become what we worship. The realm of death is passing, not permanent; men who prefer such are hollow men, for the dead praise not the Lord (Ps. 115:17). Dead in trespasses and sins (Eph. 2:1), the Chaldean is an alien from the commonwealth of Israel, a stranger from the covenants of promise, having no hope, and without God in the world. He is a walking dead man, not yet buried. No cologne in the world can cover up the nasty smell of walking independently of the Lord. In the land of confusion, life stinks.

**Who cannot be satisfied**. This word means "to fill to satisfaction" and is rendered in the King James Version as "to have enough." Because the Babylonian worships false gods, the things of this world, he has never had an experience with the One who is the Bread of Life and the Water of Life (Jn. 4:14; 6:48). All men were created to be worshipers, and true worship is the cry of the heart. The hunger and thirst of the inner man, the man of the spirit, will never be satisfied with anything except reality. Like the woman of Samaria who went from husband to husband (Jn. 4:16-18), Americans go from relationship to relationship, from job to job, from house to house, from city to city, from dress to dress, from diet to diet, from church to church, *ad nauseam*. Again, remember that true worship cannot be defined by the parameters of the external. There is nothing in that realm that can slake your thirst. Nothing!

**Who gathers and heaps unto himself.** The word for "gathereth" means "to receive." The word for "heapeth" means "to grasp or collect." Chaldeans love to collect things and are very proud of their collections. Their motto: "We have spared no expense!" They do it to impress others, especially other collectors. The problem is that Babylonians are rapists and plunderers on the side. Nothing is unto the Lord or for the benefit of other people. Everything revolves around the center of self. Indeed, you can't take it with you. In this life, Chaldeans find their identity in their collections. One day soon, they will stand before the Lord...all alone!

To summarize, Babylonians transgress by wine, are proud, won't stay at home, are greedy, are the walking dead, are unfulfilled, are worshipers of things. This is man without God, life without Jesus.

Now that we have clearly identified the Chaldean personality, we move on to discover the five things that God will *purge* out of us, out of our nation, out of the earth. Habakkuk saw a time when the knowledge of the glory of the Lord would cover the planet (2:14). When the fullness of His Kingdom comes, there will be no more:

1. *Panhandling politics.*

2. *Proud performances.*

3. *Pernicious preying.*

4. *Perverse partying.*

5. *Phobic phantoms.*

The Lord through the prophet begins to pronounce this taunting proverb, this public derision. The plundering Chaldean will be plundered. Ambitious schemes will be recompensed by shame. Sinful building will be repaid by destruction. The debaucher of nations will be debauched. The idolater will be forsaken by his idol.

### No More Panhandling Politics

Hab. 2:6, KJV:

*Shall not all these take up a parable against him, and a taunting proverb against him, and say, Woe to him that increaseth that which is not his! how long? and to him that ladeth himself with thick clay!*

Hab. 2:6, NIV:

*Will not all of them taunt him with ridicule and scorn, saying, "Woe to him who piles up stolen goods and makes himself wealthy by extortion! How long must this go on?"*

Hab. 2:7, KJV:

*Shall they not rise up suddenly that shall bite thee, and awake that shall vex thee, and thou shalt be for booties unto them?*

Hab. 2:7, NIV:

*Will not your debtors suddenly arise? Will they not wake up and make you tremble? Then you will become their victim.*

Hab. 2:8, KJV:

*Because thou hast spoiled many nations, all the remnant of the people shall spoil thee; because of men's blood, and for the violence of the land, of the city, and of all that dwell therein.*

Hab. 2:8, TLB:

*You have ruined many nations; now they will ruin you. You murderers! You have filled the countryside with lawlessness and all the cities too.*

Babylon had enriched herself by plundering other nations. Men soon rose in revenge to spoil her of all her booty. In our times, Russia did this very thing. Now she is drinking of her own crimes. God judges ambition. Businesses and ministries, once reputable, have been ruined. The oppressed have begun to revolt. Major religious denominations are cracking at the seams. Nationally, taxation without representation may stir up the spirit of another revolution.

Ferrar Fenton says of verses 6 and 7, "Woe to him, who is great upon loans! How long can he carry his debts? Will they not suddenly arise for their interest?" Space will not permit us to speak of America's national and international debt. Many fine publications are doing that for us. Suffice it to say that time is running out.

Historically, Habakkuk's word has already come to pass. Less than 25 years after Nebuchadnezzar's death in 562 B.C., Cyrus the Persian rose up "suddenly," took Babylon, and made it a province of his vast kingdom.

Men today heap up wealth, riches, and property that is not theirs. They load themselves with pledges and usury contrary to the law (Deut. 24:10). "Suddenly" these thieves will be called upon to relinquish their ill-gotten gain (1 Thess. 5:1-4). Sadly, this politicking is not confined to Washington, D.C. It lurks in the homes and churches of our land. Domestically, lives are damaged by divorce, wealth by extortion and community property law; in the church world, groups split and sheep and buildings are stolen. How long will this go on?

The word for "taunting" in verse 6 means "a satire" and is taken from a root meaning "to make mouths at, to scoff." The mockers will be mocked. The spoiler will be spoiled. The Chaldean has made himself "heavy" with "thick clay," literally "something pledged or pawned, lent on security." The heavy pawns and humiliating pledges exacted by the Chaldean from his conquered enemies will change into a mass of mud from which he cannot extricate himself. Politicians are sucking the pork barrel dry, their constituents but pawns in a very complex political game.

This "thick clay" of verse 6 also reveals the volume and density between the ears of men. A carnivore is a meat eater. The carnal mind is a meathead. Thickheaded. Dense. To illustrate this, the Amplified Bible addresses Nebuchadnezzar in verse 8, "Because you [king of Babylon] have plundered many nations, all who are left of the people shall plunder you... ." The king of confusion is the devil; his place of operations, the carnal mind. The apostle Paul explains:

Rom. 8:6, KJV:

*For to be carnally minded is death; but to be spiritually minded is life and peace.*

The word that Habakkuk used in verse 7 for "bite" means "to strike with a sting (as a serpent); to oppress with interest on a loan." Historically, the Medes and the Persians struck unexpectedly at the Babylonians. The conquerors were not only bitten by their subjects, but vexed or shaken violently, referring to the forceful seizure of a debtor by his creditor (Mt. 18:28). The Chaldeans would become "booty" or plunder to those whom they had oppressed. It's going to get interesting as God continues to deal with America through the economy.

In verse 8, the word for "spoil" means "to drop or strip, to plunder." The word for "violence" means "wrong; unjust gain; to maltreat." This is a season of reward. Those who have sown to the Spirit are enjoying the blessings of the Lord. Those who have planted an unholy crop must face the inevitable. Throughout the earth, men are reaping what they have sown. In politics, in the home, in the church, many have continued to work their wiles on the innocent. Payday is today. God now begins to purge our nation and the Church of these panhandlers and their tactics.

Gal. 6:7, KJV:

*Be not deceived; God is not mocked: for whatsoever a man soweth, that shall he also reap.*

### No More Proud Performances

Hab. 2:9, KJV:

*Woe to him that coveteth an evil covetousness to his house, that he may set his nest on high, that he may be delivered from the power of evil!*

Hab. 2:9, TLB:

*Woe to you for getting rich by evil means, attempting to live beyond the reach of danger.*

Hab. 2:10, KJV:

*Thou hast consulted shame to thy house by cutting off many people, and hast sinned against thy soul.*

Hab. 2:10, NIV:

*You have plotted the ruin of many peoples, shaming your own house and forfeiting your life.*

Hab. 2:11, KJV:

*For the stone shall cry out of the wall, and the beam out of the timber shall answer it.*

These verses tell of the Chaldean acts of tearing down other people's homes to build their palaces, other people's plants to build their own industries, other people's rights and freedoms to build their own civilization. All that they built toppled down around them, their structures witnessing against them. The covetous man inflicts personal injury and brings social disgrace.

The phrase "coveteth an evil covetousness" in verse 9 is literally "cuts an evil cut." The Chaldean makes sure he gets his "cut" of the loot. He thinks that he is immune from the "power," the "hand or grasp" of evil, disaster, or overthrow. He's stacked the deck in his favor.

Pride, the root of covetousness, lusts for possessions at the expense of others. The stones and the beams of the house would testify against such arrogance. The word for "covetousness" in verse 9 means "unjust gain." The basic meaning of "evil gain" is "breaking off," as some unethical merchants in the Orient do with pieces of silver and other metals in money transactions.

Like ancient Edom, the Chaldeans set up their government on a basis secure from attack. The imagery is that of an eagle (Job 39:37; Jer. 49:16; Obad. 4). The ungodly oppressor may think his position to be impregnable, but he has sinned and will cause his own ruin. The buildings that he has erected to his own glory and for the satisfaction of his own pride will cry out for injustices done.

The word for "consulted" in verse 10 means "to advise; to deliberate or resolve." Two frustrated and conniving wives over morning coffee, the think tanks of corporate takeovers, the smoke-filled back rooms of political conventions, the secret meetings of the deacon board—the curtain is about to fall on these proud performances. Preachers with electric suits, spiritual prima donnas with hour-long sound checks, religious conventions and groups trafficking their wares—this damnable day of competition and grading each other is about over.

Verses 9-11 describe the spirit behind all politics and denominationalism. Project after useless government project, paid for by our tax money, now raise their voice in protest. Many megachurches are in trouble. Buildings that men have built in their own name have begun to cry out for vengeance, having been financed by bleeding the life out of the real stones, the people of God. The picture here is a house struck by a sudden whirlwind and gutted by fire, a spiritual Hurricane Andrew.

Nebuchadnezzar, your kingdom is coming down. Babylon, at whose name the world once trembled, is now marked on the maps and indexes of most encyclopedias with the notation, "Babylon, Ruins of." On the Baghdad railroad it is a whistle stop for archaeologists!

Is. 14:4, KJV:

*That thou shalt take up this proverb against the king of Babylon, and say, How hath the oppressor ceased! the golden city ceased!*

*The Lord hath broken the staff of the wicked, and the sceptre of the rulers.*

Is. 14:13-15, KJV:

*For thou hast said in thine heart, I will ascend into heaven, I will exalt my throne above the stars of God: I will sit also upon the mount of the congregation, in the sides of the north:*

*I will ascend above the heights of the clouds; I will be like the most High.*

*Yet thou shalt be brought down to hell, to the sides of the pit.*

### No More Pernicious Preying

Hab. 2:12, KJV:

*Woe to him that buildeth a town with blood, and stablisheth a city by iniquity!*

Hab. 2:12, NIV:

*Woe to him who builds a city with bloodshed and establishes a town by crime!*

Hab. 2:12, TLB:

*Woe to you who build cities with money gained from murdering and robbery!*

Hab. 2:13, KJV:

*Behold, is it not of the Lord of hosts that the people shall labour in the very fire, and the people shall weary themselves for very vanity?*

Hab. 2:13, NIV:

*Has not the Lord Almighty determined that the people's labor is only fuel for the fire, that the nations exhaust themselves for nothing?*

Hab. 2:13, TLB:

*Has not the Lord decreed that godless nations' gains will turn to ashes in their hands? They work so hard, but all in vain!*

Babylon was a city of blood. Babylonian cities were built by blood. The Chaldeans had established their nation by crime, murder, and war, plundering homes and families. This third woe is against violence, the inflicting of cruel sufferings on the subjugated. Jehovah's judgment was that the very cities so built would be destroyed. Captive labor was used to build the great structures of the empire. But the work was for nought—it was all destined for the fire. By His mighty hand, God frustrated their aims and consumed their materials.

Ps. 127:1, KJV:

*Except the Lord build the house, they labour in vain that build it: except the Lord keep the city, the watchman waketh but in vain.*

Whether this "house" or "city" is political or religious, we note three things about it:

1. *It was built with the wrong materials.*
2. *The builders of it labored in vain.*
3. *It was to eventually be destroyed.*

The word for "blood" in Habakkuk 2:12 is "bloodshed." The word for "stablisheth" means "to set up." The word "city" here can refer to the state and municipal governments across America corrupted by greedy men who prey upon others.

The "city" in the New Testament is used to refer to the Church (see Mt. 5:14; Heb. 11:10; 12:22-24; Rev. 21). Denominations and non-denominational "denominations" are built by the shedding of blood, the life of the saints. It is heart-rending to understand that these man-made religious systems are doomed, that the faithful ones who built them have poured out their time, talent, and tithe into the all-reducing fire. What a waste! To build such monstrosities by "iniquity" is to raise them up by means of "moral evil or moral distortion."

Whether the machine is political or religious, the people "labour" to give it life. This word in verse 13 means "to gasp; to be exhausted, to tire, to toil" (see Ps. 6:6; 69:3; Eccles. 10:15; Is. 40:30; 47:12; and Jer. 51:58). One is reminded of the words of our Lord:

Mt. 11:28-30, KJV:

*Come unto Me, all ye that labour and are heavy laden, and I will give you rest.*

*Take My yoke upon you, and learn of Me; for I am meek and lowly in heart: and ye shall find rest unto your souls.*

*For My yoke is easy, and My burden is light.*

Similar to the Hebrew, the Greek word here means "to labor to the point of exhaustion; to feel fatigue, to work hard; to reduce strength; pains." Such is the lot of those who labor in Babylon, the nation of confusion. The word for "weary" in Habakkuk 2:13 means "to tire (as if from wearisome flight)." Yet all is for vanity, or nothing.

At this point, the prophet could have gotten depressed. His own nation was about to be plundered by a nation that would eventually be spoiled as well. Suddenly, the realm of the Spirit opened wide, lifting the seer above and beyond his time. He knew that the vision was for an "appointed time," or for the festival. In a moment, the full panoramic splendor of the Feast of Tabernacles blinded the prophet to all else. He saw something greater than Judah and Babylon, than Jehoiakim or Nebuchadnezzar, than America or its new administration. He saw the Lord of the whole earth!

### Interlude

Jehovah whispered to His servant, "Son, it doesn't matter what it looks like right now in your nation. I see the end from the beginning, and all My purposes start at the finish. I want to show you what the whole earth looks like to Me all the time!"

Hab. 2:14, KJV:

*For the earth shall be filled with the knowledge of the glory of the Lord, as the waters cover the sea.*

Hab. 2:14, TLB:

*(The time will come when all the earth is filled, as the waters fill the sea, with an awareness of the glory of the Lord.)*

These marvelous words are rehearsed throughout the Bible. When God wants to emphasize something, He repeats Himself! Compare Habakkuk 3:3 and these other key passages:

Hab. 3:3, KJV:

*God came from Teman, and the Holy One from mount Paran. Selah. His glory covered the heavens, and the earth was full of His praise.*

Num. 14:21, KJV:

*But as truly as I live, all the earth shall be filled with the glory of the Lord.*

Is. 6:3, KJV:

*And one cried unto another, and said, Holy, holy, holy, is the Lord of hosts: the whole earth is full of His glory.*

Is. 11:9, KJV:

*They shall not hurt nor destroy in all My holy mountain: for the earth shall be full of the knowledge of the Lord, as the waters cover the sea.*

Ezek. 43:2, KJV:

*And, behold, the glory of the God of Israel came from the way of the east: and His voice was like a noise of many waters: and the earth shined with His glory.*

2 Cor. 4:6, KJV:

*For God, who commanded the light to shine out of darkness, hath shined in our hearts, to give the light of the knowledge of the glory of God in the face of Jesus Christ.*

Rev. 18:1, KJV:

*And after these things I saw another angel come down from heaven, having great power; and the earth was lightened with his glory.*

Habakkuk 2:14 stands in total contrast to the preceding verses. Unlike the Chaldean and his methods, the Lord is going to establish His Kingdom with the sceptre of righteousness (Heb. 1:8-9). Then no one will hurt or destroy in all His holy mountain. When His Kingdom is established, all other kingdoms will fall (Is. 2:12-21; 11:9; Dan. 2:44).

A kingdom had been set up in Babylon to usurp power and glory (Gen. 10:10; 11:4), but it must pass away and be replaced by God's Kingdom (Rev. 11:15). In order for the earth to be filled with the knowledge of the glory of the Lord, the kingdoms and rulers of this world must be purged and judged.

This "knowledge" in verse 14 is relationship knowledge (Eph. 4:13). It means "to ascertain by seeing." This knowledge is based on vision, and Habakkuk saw the Lord. To see the Lord is to know and understand Him (Eph. 1:18).

The Hebrew word for "glory" is *kâbôd* (kaw-bode) and means "weight; splendor or copiousness." It comes from a root meaning "to be heavy; in a good sense, to be numerous, rich, or honorable." *Vine's Dictionary* adds that *kâbôd* means "great quantity, multitude, wealth, reputation (majesty), dignity" (W.E. Vine, *Vine's Expository Dictionary of Old and New Testament Words*, Old Tappan, NJ: Fleming H. Revell Co., 1981).

In the church world, we don't need to *count* the saints; we need to *weigh* them. The glory of the Lord is weighty, substantial; it is that which is real. In the Day of the Lord, this glory will "cover" the earth, literally, "fill up the hollows."

Every empty person, place, or thing will be impacted by His presence. Thus is revealed:

1. *The depth of His glory.*
2. *The abundance of His glory.*
3. *The permanence of His glory.*

Ps. 72:17-19, KJV:

*His name shall endure for ever: His name shall be continued as long as the sun: and men shall be blessed in Him: all nations shall call Him blessed.*

*Blessed be the Lord God, the God of Israel, who only doeth wondrous things.*

*And blessed be His glorious name for ever: and let the whole earth be filled with His glory; Amen, and Amen.*

In order for that day to become a reality, the five sins of the Chaldeans must be *purged* from the earth, nationally and individually. God continues to come to America and the Church in America as He deals with our hearts. After this glorious interlude, Habakkuk continues to speak to the sins of Judah.

### No More Perverse Partying

Hab. 2:15, KJV:

*Woe unto him that giveth his neighbour drink, that puttest thy bottle to him, and makest him drunken also, that thou mayest look on their nakedness!*

Hab. 2:15, TLB:

*Woe to you for making your neighboring lands reel and stagger like drunkards beneath your blows, and then gloating over their nakedness and shame.*

Hab. 2:16, KJV:

*Thou art filled with shame for glory: drink thou also, and let thy foreskin be uncovered: the cup of the Lord's right hand shall be turned unto thee, and shameful spewing shall be on thy glory.*

Hab. 2:16, NIV:

*You will be filled with shame instead of glory. Now it is your turn! Drink and be exposed! The cup from the Lord's right hand is coming around to you, and disgrace will cover your glory.*

Hab. 2:16, NKJ:

*You are filled with shame instead of glory. You also—drink! And be exposed as uncircumcised! The cup of the Lord's right hand will be turned against you, and utter shame will be on your glory.*

Hab. 2:16, Ferrar Fenton:

*You gorge on disgrace more than honour!*

Hab. 2:17, KJV:

*For the violence of Lebanon shall cover thee, and the spoil of beasts, which made them afraid, because of men's blood, and for the violence of the land, of the city, and of all that dwell therein.*

Hab. 2:17, TLB:

*You cut down the forests of Lebanon—now you will be cut down! You terrified the wild animals you caught*

*in your traps—now terror will strike you because of all*
*your murdering and violence in cities everywhere.*

"Woe unto him that giveth his neighbour drink!"
That's a sobering verse for every bartender, not to mention any adult who has ever bought a six-pack or a bottle
of wine for a teenager! Drinking, socially and otherwise,
is the accepted norm in America. Many of God's people
are snared with this problem. *Cheers* was a top-rated sit-
com. Our young people are blitzed with one commercial
after another encouraging them to drink beer, light or
otherwise. That first taste, that first sip, is the biggest
one. Major sports teams and corporations are fully aware
of that when they make their appeals.

This filthy package of poison comes disguised as the
"happy hour" at your "friendly" neighborhood tavern or
pub. In mainstream America, it's okay to drink. But ask
any woman who has had to experience an alcoholic father, husband, son, or brother, and you'll hear a different
story. Sadder still is the sight of a drunken woman.

It is demoralizing to allow oneself to come under the
stupor of drink so that a person ceases to be accountable
for his conduct. Greater yet is the sin of the man who
compels his neighbor to drink with the intent of doing
him moral harm. Take heed, America! The bottle of wine
becomes a cup of wrath, a cup of riot and retribution.

How many teenage girls have lost their virginity at
the hands of some young man with hormone problems
because they took one too many drinks? How many young
people are killed each year by drunk drivers? Mothers
are mad, but God is going to solve the problem. The party

is about to be over. Insolence and brutality are magnified by the use of alcohol and drugs. LSD is coming back on the scene. Didn't we learn anything in the 60s?

In Scripture, the condition of a drunken man represents the overthrow of a conquered nation (Nahum 3:11). Yet tobacco, alcohol, and drugs remain billion-dollar industries in America. For Babylon's sin in Habakkuk's day, foul shame would come upon the Chaldeans. They would be as the uncircumcised, the height of contempt. They would drink the cup they had made others to drink (Jer. 25:15).

Woe to him that "irrigates or furnishes a portion to." This word in Habakkuk 2:15 is rendered as "cause to drink or drown" in the King James Version. God has reserved a special judgment for natural and spiritual bartenders. Churches throughout the land have abused the gifts of the Holy Spirit in the name of a "good time" in the Lord (Is. 28:1-8). We sing and shout a lot, but the Bible must be taught and lived.

Men can't drown their sorrows; Jesus has already carried them (Is. 53:3-4). The word for "drunken" in verse 15 means "to become tipsy; to satiate with a stimulating drink or influence." You name it, and Americans are drunk on it. Sex, sports, money, power, even "church"—all these things have made us numb. Why do men do it? That they may "look intently" on the nakedness of each other, literally and figuratively.

Because of perverse partying, our college campuses are filled with "shame" and "disgrace." This word in verse 16 can be translated as "confusion, dishonor, and reproach." Drink and be "exposed!" is a principle. It means "to strip; to go naked; figuratively, to refrain from using." Young man, young lady, do you want to waste your gifts and talents, to blow your education? Then keep on partying every weekend. As you shamefully spew in the natural (the Hebrew word means "an intense disgrace"), God will spew you out of His mouth (Rev. 3:16). You will become an intense disgrace to yourself and your family. It's not worth it. Use your gifts and talents for the glory of God. Go through life with a testimony of value (Ps. 23).

Contrast Habakkuk 2:17 with 2:14. The word for "cover" is the same. In the 90s, we will be covered with either "violence" or "glory." We will be drunk on the earthy wine of sensuality or the wine of the Holy Spirit (Song 2:4; Ps. 16:11; Eph. 5:17-18). The word for "spoil" means "to ravage or devastate." That's the partying spirit. Spring break can kill you.

In the churches of America, there are two things that are killing the seed of the Word of God: legalism and license, or law and lust. Paul dealt with both in his epistle to the Galatians as he exposed the Judaizers and the Antinomians. Legalism will kill you. License will kill you quicker. Classical Pentecostalism in America was and is marked by legalism. Those of us who escaped that cage were so glad to get out that we got up a full head of steam, ran across the road, and fell headlong into the other ditch. In the Charismatic Renewal, there was no government. We did as we felt "led" to do. Now anything goes, for us and for our children. In the 90s, God is calling the Church back to a genuine personal holiness. The party's over. It's time to go home.

The most famous party in the Bible is found in the fifth chapter of the Book of Daniel. Belshazzar, grandson of Nebuchadnezzar, got drunk with his lords and ran to excess (Rom. 13:11-14; Gal. 5:21). As then, the handwriting is on the wall, but nobody can read it. America loves to party. Christians from every quarter want the benefits without the procedure. We want to eat, drink, and be merry!

We live in denial. We want buzzed and bombed, to escape our problems. Like Habakkuk, Daniel was a real prophet. We have been weighed in the balances and found wanting. Who wants to be third ruler in a kingdom that won't be here in the morning? The designated Driver for the rest of the evening is the Lord Himself. He's the only One who can get us back to the House safely.

Lk. 21:34, KJV:

*And take heed to yourselves, lest at any time your hearts be overcharged with surfeiting, and drunkenness, and cares of this life, and so that day come upon you unawares.*

## No More Phobic Phantoms

Hab. 2:18, KJV:

*What profiteth the graven image that the maker thereof hath graven it; the molten image, and a teacher of lies, that the maker of his work trusteth therein, to make dumb idols?*

Hab. 2:18, NIV:

*Of what value is an idol, since a man has carved it? Or an image that teaches lies? For he who makes it trusts in his own creation; he makes idols that cannot speak.*

Hab. 2:18, NKJ:

*What profit is the image, that its maker should carve it, the molded image, a teacher of lies, that the maker of its mold should trust in it, to make mute idols?*

Hab. 2:18, TLB:

*What profit was there in worshiping all your man-made idols? What a foolish lie that they could help! What fools you were to trust what you yourselves had made.*

Hab. 2:19, KJV:

*Woe unto him that saith to the wood, Awake; to the dumb stone, Arise, it shall teach! Behold, it is laid over with gold and silver, and there is no breath at all in the midst of it.*

Hab. 2:19, NIV:

*Woe to him who says to wood, "Come to life!" Or to lifeless stone, "Wake up!" Can it give guidance? It is covered with gold and silver; there is no breath in it.*

Hab. 2:19, TLB:

*Woe to those who command their lifeless wooden idols to arise and save them, who call out to the speechless stone to tell them what to do. Can images speak for God? They are overlaid with gold and silver, but there is no breath at all inside!*

This fifth and final condemnation fell upon those who had created their own helpless gods, "dumb idols"—literally, "dumb nothings." The description here is wholly satirical, mocking the gods who cannot answer (1 Kings 18:26-29). This last woe is uttered upon the greatest sin of all: idolatry.

Religious superstition and the spirit of fear create these phobic phantoms. The Concordant Version of the Old Testament calls them "apparitions." The teacher of lies is the idol because of the false oracles connected to its worship. The idol may be overlaid with the earthly splendor of silver and gold, but there is no life within it. No Spirit exists within its breast. The apostle Paul said the same thing to the church at Corinth.

1 Cor. 12:1-3, KJV:

> *Now concerning spiritual gifts, brethren, I would not have you ignorant.*
>
> *Ye know that ye were Gentiles, carried away unto these dumb idols, even as ye were led.*
>
> *Wherefore I give you to understand, that no man speaking by the Spirit of God calleth Jesus accursed: and that no man can say that Jesus is the Lord, but by the Holy Ghost.*

The Greek word for "dumb" here is *aphonos* and means "voiceless, mute; without sound; unmeaning." These lifeless images come in many packages, for man can worship anything or anyone. Idols can take the form of literal images and statues, nature and the environment, psychic phenomena, or the stars (astral, Hollywood, sports, rock music). In the church world, it can be a preacher who is seminary-trained but has never had a life-changing experience with the One who wrote the Bible. These are all dumb asses "speaking with man's voice" (2 Pet. 2:16).

Every Sunday, millions of Americans fellowship the back of somebody's head in a dead church listening to a man without the Holy Ghost behind the "sacred desk." All they ever hear is a sin-conscious gospel, "another gospel" (Gal. 1:6-8). Christ is not preached. The congregation is left in the lower state of "how long" and "why," knowing nothing of the watchtower, the place of heavenly vision and understanding. The idol proclaims, "Hold on! Jesus will come at any minute and all our troubles will be over. We'll understand it better by and by." We need to understand it now!

A man who is not filled with the Holy Ghost has no spiritual sense. As Christians, we have no right to make decisions without the guidance of the Holy Ghost. Some parents are crazy enough to let Junior make decisions without the Holy Ghost, but Junior doesn't know what he wants. He lives in the land of "how long" and "why." He hasn't been up to the watchtower...he doesn't know that he has one! No one ever taught him how to pray.

Any and all idolatry is a system of lies, impotence, and vanity. An idol is anyone or anything men put ahead of the Lord. It's easy to know what our idols are:

1. *What we think about the most.*
2. *What we talk about the most.*
3. *That upon which we spend the most.*

The prophet gets right to the point. "What profit or value are these phantoms?" The word for "maker" in Habakkuk 2:18 speaks of something molded into shape, especially as a potter; figuratively, it means "to determine, or form a resolution." Make no mistake about it. The lord of darkness has a plan to destroy this nation; his major target is our youth, the seed, our heritage. Through the spirit of fear, the "maker" of every idol, the devil, has deceived the whole world (Rev. 12:9).

Who's behind the scenes making your career, your marriage, your ministry? The Potter from Heaven or the potter from hell (Jer. 18; Eph. 2:1-3)?

Each of these idols is a teacher of "lies"—literally, "an untruth or sham." This word comes from a root meaning "to cheat; be untrue (usually in words)." Truth is reality. The Bible, the Word of God, is Truth (Jn. 17:17). Jesus Christ is Truth (Jn. 14:6). The Holy Spirit is the Spirit of Truth (Jn. 16:13; 1 John 2:27).

Anything outside of the Christ nature is a lying vanity. Christ is the "image of God" (2 Cor. 4:4). Parents, what do you see when you look at your children? Pastors, what do you see when you look at the saints? My fellow citizens, what do you see when you look at America?

How do you deal with people? From the earthly view of "how long" and "why," or from the Lord's perspective? If patience is a fruit of the Spirit (Gal. 5:22-23), then impatience is the work of the flesh. An anxious parent asks, "Lord, why have You placed this 'hyper, over-abundant, full-of-energy, won't-sit-down, and won't-be-quiet' little boy or girl under my roof? He is a holy terror (like the Chaldeans)!" How do you see him? With your brain?

Forget it. Get on the watchtower and begin to prophesy about his "earth" (2:14)!

Christ is the image of God. Antichrist is any other image, the wrong image. When we deal with others on the basis of the lower image, we teach lies. We tend to assume and presume the worst rather than best about each other. Whose report will you believe (Is. 53:1)? We must believe the report of the Lord. Some still ask, "Lord, I don't understand where You're coming from." We're about to find that out (Hab. 3:3).

These phantoms live between men's ears and haunt the houses of the unredeemed. All have their roots in the spirit of fear. This is seen in the word for "work" in verse 18. It means "a form or conception" and is rendered in the King James Version as "frame, thing framed, imagination, mind, or work." In the Old Testament, these idols were built and worshiped in the "high places." Paul explains "every high thing" in the New Testament.

2 Cor. 10:4-5, KJV:

*(For the weapons of our warfare are not carnal, but mighty through God to the pulling down of strong holds;)*

*Casting down imaginations, and every high thing that exalteth itself against the knowledge of God, and bringing into captivity every thought to the obedience of Christ.*

2 Cor. 10:4-5, NIV:

*The weapons we fight with are not the weapons of the world. On the contrary, they have divine power to demolish strongholds.*

*We demolish arguments and every pretension that sets itself up against the knowledge of God, and we take captive every thought to make it obedient to Christ.*

In the 90s, we will not be able to "trust" or "flee for refuge" to these things. We cannot continue to put our trust and confidence in that which has no life. These lesser gods are "dumb" idols. This word in Habakkuk 2:19 means "speechless or tongue-tied." The word for "idol" itself means that which is "good for nothing; vain or vanity; no value." The prophet Isaiah has some good advice for America.

Is. 55:2, NIV:

*Why spend money on what is not bread, and your labor on what does not satisfy? Listen, listen to Me, and eat what is good, and your soul will delight in the richest of fare.*

The wood and the stone are "dumb." Men were designed to hear and do the Word of the Lord. The word for "dumb" in verse 19 is different than the word in the preceding verse. Here it refers to that which is "still" and is taken from a root revealing that the idol was "astonished" and made to "stop" its speech. This is the Day of the Lord. He is speaking now. Everything without "breath," not energized by His *Ruach*, His "Spirit," is made speechless, void of power. Let us renounce our idols and call upon the name of the Lord. Only He can deliver us.

## After the Purging

The last verse of this chapter pictures the Divine court. God resides there, governing the universe, demanding silence in His presence. He is the Judge of all.

Habakkuk's fivefold denunciation came to pass. God purged Babylon from the face of the earth in the sixth century B.C. He is cleansing America and the nations now, having begun a global baptism of fire. The elements, those rudimentary concepts and principles which have formed the basis for a man-centered life style, are beginning to melt with "fervent heat" (2 Pet. 3:7-13). This fire is His Word through the mouth of His true servants (Jer. 23:29; Jn. 1:1; Heb. 12:29). This day is the Day of the Lord, and is typified in Scripture by the Feast Day of Atonement (Lev. 16), preparing the nations for the harvest Feast of Tabernacles.

God has come to America. Apostles and prophets are being sent from the Lord to speak His Word concerning our politicking, our pride, our preying (not praying), our partying, and our phantoms (idols). Once He has dealt with this nation and the nations, we can say with Habakkuk:

Hab. 2:20, KJV:

*But the Lord is in His holy temple: let all the earth keep silence before Him.*

Hab. 2:20, AMP:

*...let all the earth hush...*

Hab. 2:20, Moffatt:

*But the Eternal is within His sacred temple; hush, all men, He is here!*

Hab. 2:20, Ferrar Fenton:

*But the Lord is in His holy home; let the earth in His presence be still!*

This thought is conveyed by the words of two other prophets, David and Micah:

Ps. 11:4, KJV:

*The Lord is in His holy temple, the Lord's throne is in heaven: His eyes behold, His eyelids try, the children of men.*

Mic. 1:2, KJV:

*Hear, all ye people; hearken, O earth, and all that therein is: and let the Lord God be witness against you, the Lord from His holy temple.*

Habakkuk had begun with a sigh. Now all is at rest. His questions had been answered. God is on the scene. God is at home. The prophet himself is the temple of the Lord!

1 Cor. 3:16, KJV:

*Know ye not that ye are the temple of God, and that the Spirit of God dwelleth in you?*

2 Cor. 6:16, KJV:

*And what agreement hath the temple of God with idols? for ye are the temple of the living God; as God hath said, I will dwell in them, and walk in them; and I will be their God, and they shall be My people.*

Col. 1:27, KJV:

*To whom God would make known what is the riches of the glory of this mystery among the Gentiles; which is Christ in you, the hope of glory.*

Eph. 3:17, KJV:

*That Christ may dwell in your hearts by faith; that ye, being rooted and grounded in love....*

The prophet's sob was about to become a song. He could now embrace the ways of the Lord because he had embraced the Lord Himself. His eyes had been opened. He had seen the Messiah! Worry gave way to worship. He could sing:

Turn your eyes upon Jesus.
Look full in His wonderful face,
And the things of earth will grow strangely dim
In the light of His glory and grace!

Habakkuk found the solution; he unlocked the secret. The apparent strength of wickedness is false. The Lord reigns. There is a bigger picture that rises far above present circumstances. It's bigger than Judah or Babylon. It's bigger than the new administration and the problems of America. It's bigger than the economy, immorality, and violence. It's bigger than anything that has you upset right now. It's bigger than your "earth."

Mt. 4:10, KJV:

*Then saith Jesus unto him, Get thee hence, Satan: for it is written, Thou shalt worship the Lord thy God, and Him only shalt thou serve.*

The root word for "temple" in Habakkuk 2:20 means "to be able." That says it all. That's the bottom line for the 90s. Only God is able to carry us through. Everything else is losing its strength. The only ones who speak in the Divine court are the Father, the Judge, and the Son, our Advocate (1 John 2:1). The voice of man is not heard in this Most Holy Place. The word for "keep silence" in verse 20 means "to hush." It is used elsewhere in the Old Testament in these verses:

Num. 13:30, KJV:

*And Caleb stilled the people before Moses, and said, Let us go up at once, and possess it; for we are well able to overcome it.*

Neh. 8:11, KJV:

*So the Levites stilled all the people, saying, Hold your peace, for the day is holy; neither be ye grieved.*

Zeph. 1:7, KJV:

*Hold thy peace at the presence of the Lord God: for the day of the Lord is at hand: for the Lord hath prepared a sacrifice, He hath bid His guests.*

Zech. 2:13, KJV:

*Be silent, O all flesh, before the Lord: for He is raised up out of His holy habitation.*

God is in control. Nothing can disturb you if the Lord is at home. Let all the earth keep silence. Be quiet. The time is coming when every nation will turn to the Lord and trust Him. Our King not only shuts the mouth of the lion; He also causes us to "rest in the day of trouble"! Be still, and know that He is God!

Habakkuk had seen three bright stars, three immutable absolutes, in this second chapter of his prophecy:

1. *The just shall live by His faith (2:4).*
2. *The earth shall be filled with the knowledge of His glory (2:14).*
3. *The Lord is in His holy temple (2:20).*

There is new hope for America and the world! Once a man sees the Lord, all he can do is sing. There is a sovereign God ruling both the earth and the universe. His Kingdom rules over all!

But He's so big! How can we begin to understand Him? Six hundred years before it happened, Habakkuk saw the focal point of redemption's plan. The vision before him was life-changing. Creation's sob becomes creation's song. Let's closely examine his glorious revelation. What this prophet saw is a real answer for America. More to the point, it's a real answer for *you!*

# PART THREE:
# THE PRAYER

## Singing Faith

## Chapter Seven

# The Provision

### "God came from Teman"

### Habakkuk 3:1-3

Hab. 3:1-3, KJV:

*A prayer of Habakkuk the prophet upon Shigionoth.*

*O Lord, I have heard Thy speech, and was afraid: O Lord, revive Thy work in the midst of the years, in the midst of the years make known; in wrath remember mercy.*

*God came from Teman, and the Holy One from mount Paran. Selah. His glory covered the heavens, and the earth was full of His praise.*

"Let all the earth keep silence before Him."

The sovereign God was on His throne, just and holy. The Judge of all the earth had decreed the verdict. The prophet had no more questions, no more reasonings. Submission was complete. Habakkuk was at rest in the day of trouble. The Levite now opens his lips in adoration and praise to the Chief Singer. If there is any request at all, it is for mercy.

Habakkuk's heart was deeply moved. Like Isaiah and Daniel, he had seen and "embraced" the Lord. Transcendent prayer had birthed this grand and glorious vision. The mood of death and depression had been swallowed up by the Lord's answer. God's *provision* was enough. There was nothing to do now but sing!

Scriptural parallels to this poem are found in Deuteronomy 33:2-5; Judges 5:4-5; Psalms 68:7-8; 77:13-20; 114:1-8; and Isaiah 63:11-14. Read them with this third chapter as you meditate the greatness of our God.

There are two kinds of people in America: unbelievers and believers; tares and wheat; those who are sobbing and those who are singing...singing before the band begins to play, singing all the time (Eph. 5:19-21).

Hab. 3:1, KJV:

> *A prayer of Habakkuk the prophet upon Shigionoth.*

Hab. 3:1, TLB:

> *This is the prayer of triumph that Habakkuk sang before the Lord:*

Hab. 3:1, ASV:

> *A prayer of Habakkuk the prophet, set to Shigionoth.*

Chapter 3 is a prayer in the form of a psalm to be sung by the Levites in the temple service (1 Chron. 25:1-8). This is obvious from the superscription ("upon Shigionoth"), the "selahs" (3:3,9,13) and the subscription ("to the chief singer on my stringed instruments").

This third chapter is actually a prayerful song, a prayer set to music. The word for "prayer" is *tephillâh* and means "intercession, supplication; by implication, a hymn." Its root *pâlal* means "to judge; to intercede, pray." This kind of song releases the judicial authority of the King and His Kingdom! In Judah ("praise") is God known (Ps. 76:1).

Used as liturgy for the formal worship service, *tephillâh* is the title for five of the Psalms (17, 86, 90, 102, 142). This prayer of Habakkuk was the Song of the Lord, or a "spiritual song" (Eph. 5:19) birthed by the Holy Spirit. Note the first use of *tephillâh* in the Old Testament with other key passages.

2 Sam. 7:27, KJV:

*For Thou, O Lord of hosts, God of Israel, hast revealed to Thy servant, saying, I will build thee an house: therefore hath Thy servant found in his heart to pray this prayer unto Thee.*

Ps. 141:2, KJV:

*Let my prayer be set forth before Thee as incense; and the lifting up of my hands as the evening sacrifice.*

Prov. 15:8, KJV:

*The sacrifice of the wicked is an abomination to the Lord: but the prayer of the upright is His delight.*

Jon. 2:7, KJV:

*When my soul fainted within me I remembered the Lord: and my prayer came in unto Thee, into Thine holy temple.*

For the meaning of the word "prophet," see Habakkuk 1:1. For the meaning and significance of "Shigionoth," see the Epilogue, the last chapter and summary of this whole volume.

Hab. 3:2, KJV:

*O Lord, I have heard Thy speech, and was afraid: O Lord, revive Thy work in the midst of the years, in the midst of the years make known; in wrath remember mercy.*

Hab. 3:2, NIV:

*Lord, I have heard of Your fame; I stand in awe of Your deeds, O Lord. Renew them in our day, in our time make them known; in wrath remember mercy.*

Hab. 3:2, TLB:

*O Lord, now I have heard Your report, and I worship You in awe for the fearful things You are going to do. In this time of our deep need, begin again to help us, as You did in years gone by. Show us Your power to save us. In Your wrath, remember mercy.*

Habakkuk had heard the Lord's report. It was necessary for his beloved nation to be chastened, to go into captivity. He could not pray for deliverance *from* these things, so he prayed that God would give them sufficient grace *in* these things. If Jehovah would not withdraw His correction to Judah, then the prophet's prayer was that the Lord would not withdraw Himself. The only real hope for America or any nation is the manifest presence of God in the midst of her people. Apart from this *provision* of divine life and glory, we are doomed.

The greatest blessing in your life is that you can still hear. A man's first priority is to learn how to recognize the voice of the Lord. His second is to impart that grace to his seed, his natural and spiritual children.

The word for "heard" in Habakkuk 3:2 means "to hear intelligently, often with the implication of attention and obedience." The prophet had learned to hear God's "speech" with his heart, not just his head. This word means "something heard; a sound or announcement; a report." God still speaks to men today. This certain sound from the Most Holy Place is heard only by those whose heart is toward the One who is speaking.

The word for "afraid" here can mean "alarm." Habakkuk was over-awed to hear of the coming judgment upon Judah through the Chaldeans, and then upon the Chaldeans themselves. The overthrow of the empire of the world filled him with alarm at the omnipotence of the earth's Judge. The fear of the Lord is returning to the Church, and eventually to our nation. Once again men will reverence Him.

Prov. 1:7, KJV:

*The fear of the Lord is the beginning of knowledge: but fools despise wisdom and instruction.*

Prov. 9:10, KJV:

*The fear of the Lord is the beginning of wisdom: and the knowledge of the holy is understanding.*

This word for "afraid" in Habakkuk 3:2 also means "to revere." The fear of the Lord is the beginning of all knowledge and wisdom. The Lord will not be reverenced in America until He is reverenced in the Church. Habakkuk was anointed with the spirit of the fear of the Lord (Is. 11:2).

Those who see no hope for America have not seen the Lord. Such are content to "fly away" and leave this planet to the devil and his crowd. Not Habakkuk! The prophet cried for Jehovah to revive His work, literally His "acts." The great "work" of God on earth, which includes all His works, is the salvation of man through Jesus Christ (Ps. 44:1; 77:12). The prophet sees the bigger picture, including the "work" of God to save America.

Is. 64:8, KJV:

> *But now, O Lord, Thou art our father; we are the clay, and Thou our potter; and we all are the work of Thy hand.*

Habakkuk's song began with a cry for revival! Throughout the Gospels and the Book of Acts, Jesus went everywhere preaching, teaching, and healing. Our heavenly Commander-in-Chief now equips His army with a new song; we are to finish what He began to do and teach (Acts 1:1). The word for "revive" in Habakkuk 3:2 means "to live" and is translated as "recover, repair, restore (to life)" in the King James Version. It means to restore to life, to keep alive, to give life, to call to life.

There's going to be a revival in the land (see Neh. 4:2; Ps. 138:7; Is. 57:15; Hos. 6:2)! In the midst of the years, God will make Himself known (Dan. 9:24-27). In the midst of Judah's captivity of 70 years (606-536 B.C.) as prophesied by Jeremiah (Jer. 25:8-13), Jehovah began to prepare and preserve a people of restoration, a people who would return to their homeland. Ultimately, the "years" mentioned here reflect the full scope of His purpose, the beginning and end of redemption's plan (Gen. 1:26-28; Acts 3:19-21).

Ps. 74:1, KJV:

> *O God, why hast Thou cast us off for ever? why doth Thine anger smoke against the sheep of Thy pasture?*

Ps. 74:11-12, KJV:

> *Why withdrawest Thou Thy hand, even Thy right hand? pluck it out of Thy bosom.*
> *For God is my King of old, working salvation in the midst of the earth.*

But God's "wrath" came upon Judah. This word in Habakkuk 3:2 means "commotion, restlessness (of a horse), a crash (of thunder)." The contemporary Chaldeans—the economy, immorality, and violence—remind us that the wheels have come off in America and the nations. This world system is headed for the rocks (Acts 27). Yet in the midst of judgment, those who have learned Habakkuk's song will pray for "mercy," meaning "to fondle or love." We are still His children. His mercy and compassion have endured even to our generation.

Ps. 25:6, KJV:

> *Remember, O Lord, Thy tender mercies and Thy lovingkindness; for they have been ever of old.*

## The Mystery of Godliness

The prophet now begins to picture a future redemption under figures from past events. The background here is the exodus and what took place at Mount Sinai in the days of Moses. The Lord manifested Himself and redeemed Israel from 400 years of Egyptian bondage by the blood of a Passover lamb. He will appear again to deliver the godly from their oppressors and will judge their foes.

This is more than a description of a storm sweeping across the desert; it is a Theophany, an appearance of the Lord. Jehovah comes as an armed warrior with horses and chariot, bow and quiver, in storm and lightning, to overthrow the enemy. It is best to put this Theophany in the present tense, as does the Septuagint (the Greek Old Testament).

Habakkuk sees New Testament realities in the mold of Old Testament types and figures. God granted him the gift of seeing history as God Himself sees it, not bound by time and space. In one brief panoramic moment, the prophet beheld events that lie centuries and millennia apart. He sees all divine deliverances throughout all time from every form of evil as *one* grand, once-and-for-all deliverance, the spoil of that great battle of God's Anointed on Calvary's cross. From Jehovah's view, "It is finished" (Jn. 19:30).

Hab. 3:3, KJV:

> *God came from Teman, and the Holy One from mount Paran. Selah. His glory covered the heavens, and the earth was full of His praise.*

Hab. 3:3, TLB:

*I see God moving across the deserts from Mount
Sinai. His brilliant splendor fills the earth and sky; His
glory fills the heavens, and the earth is full of His
praise! What a wonderful God He is!*

Hab. 3:3, Ferrar Fenton:

*The Lord advanced from Teman, and the Holy from
Mount Paran. His glory clothed the skies, and His
grandeur filled the earth.*

This is the key verse in chapter 3. Its apostolic interpretation was given centuries later as one of the
mysteries of the New Covenant.

1 Tim. 3:16, KJV:

*And without controversy great is the mystery of
godliness: God was manifest in the flesh, justified in the
Spirit, seen of angels, preached unto the Gentiles,
believed on in the world, received up into glory.*

1 Tim. 3:16, NIV:

*Beyond all question, the mystery of godliness is
great: He appeared in a body, was vindicated by the
Spirit, was seen by angels, was preached among the nations, was believed on in the world, was taken up in glory.*

1 Tim. 3:16, TLB:

*It is quite true that the way to live a godly life is not
an easy matter. But the answer lies in Christ, who came
to earth as a man, was proved spotless and pure in His
Spirit, was served by angels, was preached among the*

*nations, was accepted by men everywhere, and was received up again to His glory in heaven.*

"I see God!" the prophet cried.

Here is the only answer for America and the nations. Here is Heaven's response to earth's cry, God's last Word on the subject. He has done all that He can do. The secret to understanding the prophet's song of faith, the Book of Habakkuk, the whole Bible, is to know that:

"God was manifest in the flesh."

"He appeared in a body."

"Christ...came to earth as a man."

"God shall come from Teman" (literal Hebrew).

First, we declare the mystery. Then, we explain the mystery. It begins with Scripture's first promise of the coming Messiah, earth's Savior and Deliverer.

Gen. 3:15, KJV:

*And I will put enmity between thee and the woman, and between thy seed and her seed; it shall bruise thy head, and thou shalt bruise his heel.*

Gen. 3:15, NIV:

*And I will put enmity between you and the woman, and between your offspring and hers; he will crush your head, and you will strike his heel."*

God came from Teman, from "Edom." (Teman was a great city in the south of Edom.)

God came from "Edom," from "Adam."

God came from man, the Seed of the woman.

Jesus Christ was God Almighty manifested in the flesh. He laid aside His preincarnate deity and non-moral attributes (the *kenosis* or "emptying" of Philippians 2:1-11) and became like us, partaking of flesh and blood.

Gal. 4:4, NIV:

*But when the time had fully come, God sent His Son, born of a woman....*

On the devil's own turf, in the nasty now and now, King Jesus defeated sin, sickness, poverty, and death *as a man* full of the Holy Ghost! He crushed every foe. Earth's song of praise is the celebration, the declaration of His eternal triumph over all our enemies (Eph. 1:20-23).

Rom. 8:20-21, NIV:

*For the creation was subjected to frustration, not by its own choice, but by the will of the one who subjected it, in hope*

*that the creation itself will be liberated from its bondage to decay and brought into the glorious freedom of the children of God.*

Before God ever lowered man into futility, He slew the Lamb (Rev. 13:8). Jesus Christ alone is our *Provision.* He has faced and overcome all that troubles this nation. Every one of America's ills can be spelled with one word: *sin.* Jesus Christ conquered sin in the flesh. He alone is the only cure and antidote for man's woes. Because of His victory, we can rest in the day of trouble.

Acts 4:12, KJV:

*Neither is there salvation in any other: for there is none other name under heaven given among men, whereby we must be saved.*

Phil. 4:19, KJV:

> *But my God shall supply all your need according to His riches in glory by Christ Jesus.*

Over 600 years before the veil in the temple would be rent (Mt. 27:51), God tore open the heavens and revealed His plan to His prophet. Habakkuk saw the Word made flesh, the birth of Jesus Christ, His incarnation. Jehovah was not to stay behind that curtain forever.

At the end of this chapter, read and meditate what both testaments have to say about the Word being made flesh, about Immanuel, "God with us." Jesus came from the seed of the woman. He came here to live among us, to live as us. He put all enemies under His feet, then sent the Holy Ghost to equip His Church to do the same thing.

Heb. 2:5-9, KJV:

> *For unto the angels hath He not put in subjection the world to come, whereof we speak.*
>
> *But one in a certain place testified, saying, What is man, that Thou art mindful of him? or the son of man, that Thou visitest him?*
>
> *Thou madest him a little lower than the angels; Thou crownedst him with glory and honour, and didst set him over the works of Thy hands:*
>
> *Thou hast put all things in subjection under his feet. For in that He put all in subjection under him, He left nothing that is not put under him. But now we see not yet all things put under him.*
>
> *But we see Jesus, who was made a little lower than the angels for the suffering of death, crowned with glory*

*and honour; that He by the grace of God should taste death for every man.*

We have declared the "mystery of godliness." To explain this mystery, we now exegete verse 3 of Habakkuk's song.

"Teman" is a person and a place in the Bible. It means "the south (as being on the right hand of a person facing the east)." It has also been translated to mean "sunny, good fortune, prosperity, abundance, good faith, firm, faithful." Its etymology goes to the root *yâman* (yaw-man), which means "to be right (firm); to be right-handed or take the right-handed side." That is most interesting in the light of Acts 2:33; Ephesians 3:20; Hebrews 8:1; and First Peter 3:22. God came from Teman, and His name was Jesus, the Faithful Witness who now sits at the right hand of the Majesty in the heavens!

Gen. 36:15, KJV:

*These were dukes of the sons of Esau: the sons of Eliphaz the firstborn son of Esau; duke Teman, duke Omar, duke Zepho, duke Kenaz...*

Jer. 49:7, KJV:

*Concerning Edom, thus saith the Lord of hosts; Is wisdom no more in Teman? is counsel perished from the prudent? is their wisdom vanished?*

"Teman" was a person, the grandson of Esau, and a place in Edom. Teman in the south and Bozrah in the north were the two great cities of Edom, Teman being protected by the mighty fortress of Petra. Teman was perhaps the capital and is used here to represent all Idumea, known also as Mount Seir.

All students of the Scripture know that both Esau and Edom represent the *flesh*. "Teman" is Edom. Edom is "Teman."

The Hebrew word for "Edom" goes back to the root *âdam* (aw-dam) (Strong's #119), which means "to show blood (in the face)" and is translated as "red or ruddy."

Edom is *Adam*. Adam is *man*. God came from Teman. God came from Adam, from t(h)e-man, from the Seed of the woman. Habakkuk saw the incarnation, the birth of Jesus Christ, the Messiah! The Word would be made flesh and tabernacle among men (Jn. 1:14).

Habakkuk calls Him "the Holy One," the One who is absolutely sovereign and exalted over all created beings. He is the sinless and pure God who hates sin. This is the God who is about to be revealed to America and the world. We will see a revival of personal holiness in the 90s. Like the Chaldeans, immorality will be judged.

This holy God comes from mount "Paran," which means "ornamental; to gleam; to explain (make clear); foliage (bright green)." Paran was a wilderness region in the central part of the Sinai peninsula (Num. 10:12; 13:26). It was west and south of Edom. First Kings 11:18 indicates that it was between Midian and Egypt.

Deut. 8:2, KJV:

> *And thou shalt remember all the way which the Lord thy God led thee these forty years in the wilderness, to humble thee, and to prove thee, to know what was in thine heart, whether thou wouldest keep His commandments, or no.*

Paran is the "wilderness," the place of testing and humility where we get to know the One who came from Teman. Habakkuk's revelation is that earth's sob becomes Heaven's song.

But you will never sing until you have sobbed! There is an order to this mystery. First you sob; then you sing. Before honor is humility; before glory comes suffering (Prov. 15:33; 1 Pet. 1:11).

This song has to be learned (Rev. 14:3). The night season, the dark hours, the precious trial of your faith, these are the classroom; loneliness, misunderstanding, and rejection are the teachers. In the depths of the human situation, we meet the God who became human and fellowship with His sufferings (Phil. 3:8-11). Weeping may endure for a night, but joy comes in the morning (Ps. 30:5). You cannot sing with Him if you haven't sobbed with Him. If we suffer with Him, we shall be glorified together (Rom. 8:17).

Deut. 33:2, KJV:

> *And he said, The Lord came from Sinai, and rose up from Seir unto them; He shined forth from mount Paran, and He came with ten thousands of saints: from His right hand went a fiery law for them.*

Paran is always linked to Sinai, and Sinai is the mountain upon which God gave Moses the Decalogue, the Ten Commandments, the Law. Jehovah is the Lawgiver, the Judge (Hab. 2:20). Sinai is the mountain of covenant. Jesus came to fulfill the Law (Mt. 5:17). The Father has committed all judgment unto the Son (Jn. 5:22). He *is* the Truth (Jn. 14:6), the embodiment of all that is righteous. He is the bright and gleaming One. He is the Vine, the Foliage of life (Jn. 15:1-5). He came to reveal the Father.

John 1:18, AMP:

*No man has ever seen God at any time; the only unique Son, the only-begotten God, Who is in the bosom (that is, in the intimate presence) of the Father, He has declared Him—He has revealed Him, brought Him out where He can be seen; He has interpreted Him, and He has made Him known.*

In Habakkuk 3:3, the prophet used language to describe the rising of the sun, the morning as it covers the heavens with light, the dawning of a new day—it prefigures a new era, a new covenant. Jesus Christ is the Daystar of the New Testament (2 Pet. 1:19). On the night that Jesus Christ was born, "His glory covered the heavens, and the earth was full of His praise!"

Lk. 2:9-14, KJV:

*And, lo, the angel of the Lord came upon them, and the glory of the Lord shone round about them: and they were sore afraid.*

*And the angel said unto them, Fear not: for, behold, I bring you good tidings of great joy, which shall be to all people.*

*For unto you is born this day in the city of David a Saviour, which is Christ the Lord.*

*And this shall be a sign unto you; Ye shall find the babe wrapped in swaddling clothes, lying in a manger.*

*And suddenly there was with the angel a multitude of the heavenly host praising God, and saying,*

*Glory to God in the highest, and on earth peace, good will toward men.*

No wonder Habakkuk said, "Selah," which means "a suspension (in the music); pause; to weigh." History's most longed-for moment, when God Almighty bundled Himself in eight pounds of love, brought a suspension in the music. God wrapped Himself in flesh; then Mary wrapped that "holy thing" in swaddling clothes and laid Him in a manger (Lk. 1:35). We must stop what we are doing and "weigh" that. The only hope for America was born long ago. That baby boy was Christ the Lord! Our Hope still lives (1 Tim. 1:1). He was born of the Spirit (Lk. 1:35). So are we. Selah...

Is. 6:3, KJV:

*And one cried unto another, and said, Holy, holy, holy, is the Lord of hosts: the whole earth is full of His glory.*

"His glory covered the heavens..."

Habakkuk uses a different word for "glory" here than in 2:14. This word is *hêwd* (Strong's #1935) and means "grandeur (an imposing form and appearance)." *Vine's Dictionary* adds "splendor, majesty, authority." Compare its usage in First Chronicles 16:27; 29:11; Psalms 96:6; and Zechariah 6:13.

However, this glory "covered" (the same as Habakkuk 2:14) the heavens. This word means "to fill up the hollows" and is the root word for "throne." Jesus came to fill the void, the empty space, in every man. He alone can slake our thirst. Money cannot buy this cup. Only the finished work of Jesus Christ, through the power of the Holy Spirit, can change a man's heart. Only God can change America (Is. 55:1-9). Only the power and authority invested in His name can prevail. He is enthroned above it all.

"And the earth was full of His praise…"

The word for "full" is also the same as in 2:14 and according to Vine means "to fill, fulfill, overflow, ordain, endow." It also has a special meaning: "to fill one's hand." The needy in America and around the world are going to be ministered to by the Lord through His people. We are to be His hand extended, reaching out to the oppressed. The Church is the embassy of His Kingdom.

Finally, the word for "praise" in Habakkuk 3:3 means "laudation; a hymn." It is taken from the root *hâlal* (hawlal) (Strong's #1984) which means "to be clear; to shine; to make a show, to boast; to be clamorously foolish; to rave, to celebrate." Vine adds that *hâlal* can be rendered as a "song of praise; praiseworthy deeds."

This is why Jesus came. Let us celebrate His coming. Immanuel…God is with us! He is our song of praise!

Hab. 2:14, KJV:

> *For the earth shall be filled with the knowledge of the glory of the Lord, as the waters cover the sea.*

### The Word Was Made Flesh

Gen. 3:15, KJV:

> *And I will put enmity between thee and the woman, and between thy seed and her seed; It shall bruise thy head, and thou shalt bruise his heel.*

Ps. 40:7, KJV:

> *Then said I, Lo, I come: in the volume of the book it is written of me…*

Is. 7:14, KJV:

*Therefore the Lord Himself shall give you a sign; Behold, a virgin shall conceive, and bear a son, and shall call His name Immanuel.*

Is. 9:6, KJV:

*For unto us a child is born, unto us a son is given: and the government shall be upon His shoulder: and His name shall be called Wonderful, Counsellor, The mighty God, The everlasting Father, The Prince of Peace.*

Ezek. 3:15, KJV:

*Then I came to them of the captivity at Telabib, that dwelt by the river of Chebar, and I sat where they sat, and remained there astonished among them seven days.*

Mic. 5:2, KJV:

*But thou, Bethlehem Ephratah, though thou be little among the thousands of Judah, yet out of thee shall He come forth unto Me that is to be ruler in Israel; whose goings forth have been from of old, from everlasting.*

Lk. 24:39, KJV:

*Behold My hands and My feet, that it is I Myself: handle Me, and see; for a spirit hath not flesh and bones, as ye see Me have.*

Jn. 1:14, KJV:

*And the Word was made flesh, and dwelt among us, (and we beheld His glory, the glory as of the only begotten of the Father,) full of grace and truth.*

Acts 2:30, KJV:

*Therefore being a prophet, and knowing that God had sworn with an oath to him, that of the fruit of his loins, according to the flesh, He would raise up Christ to sit on his throne.*

Rom. 1:3, KJV:

*Concerning His Son Jesus Christ our Lord, which was made of the seed of David according to the flesh.*

Rom. 8:3, KJV:

*For what the law could not do, in that it was weak through the flesh, God sending His own Son in the likeness of sinful flesh, and for sin, condemned sin in the flesh.*

Rom. 9:5, KJV:

*Whose are the fathers, and of whom as concerning the flesh Christ came, who is over all, God blessed for ever. Amen.*

Gal. 4:4, KJV:

*But when the fulness of the time was come, God sent forth His Son, made of a woman, made under the law.*

Phil. 2:8, KJV:

*And being found in fashion as a man, He humbled Himself, and became obedient unto death, even the death of the cross.*

Col. 1:15, KJV:

*Who is the image of the invisible God, the firstborn of every creature.*

Heb. 1:3, KJV:

*Who being the brightness of His glory, and the express image of His person, and upholding all things by the word of His power, when He had by Himself purged our sins, sat down on the right hand of the Majesty on high.*

Heb. 2:14, KJV:

*Forasmuch then as the children are partakers of flesh and blood, He also Himself likewise took part of the same; that through death He might destroy Him that had the power of death, that is, the devil.*

Heb. 2:17, KJV:

*Wherefore in all things it behoved Him to be made like unto His brethren, that He might be a merciful and faithful high priest in things pertaining to God, to make reconciliation for the sins of the people.*

Heb. 4:15, KJV:

*For we have not an high priest which cannot be touched with the feeling of our infirmities; but was in all points tempted like as we are, yet without sin.*

1 John 1:2, KJV:

*(For the life was manifested, and we have seen it, and bear witness, and shew unto you that eternal life, which was with the Father, and was manifested unto us;).*

1 John 4:2-3, KJV:

*Hereby know ye the Spirit of God: Every spirit that confesseth that Jesus Christ is come in the flesh is of God:*

> *And every spirit that confesseth not that Jesus Christ is come in the flesh is not of God: and this is that spirit of antichrist, whereof ye have heard that it should come; and even now already is it in the world.*

2 John 1:7, KJV:

> *For many deceivers are entered into the world, who confess not that Jesus Christ is come in the flesh. This is a deceiver and an antichrist.*

Rev. 22:16, KJV:

> *I Jesus have sent Mine angel to testify unto you these things in the churches. I am the root and the offspring of David, and the bright and morning star.*

No one knows the future of America or all that's coming into your life or mine. But we can rest in the confidence that God turned Habakkuk's sob into a song, his tragedy into triumph. God's faith and grace is enough (2 Cor. 12:9).

The Word was made flesh, the flesh became striped, and by His stripes we were healed (1 Pet. 2:24). God came from man so that man could go to God. He became us so that we could become like Him (2 Cor. 5:21). The Passover lamb was inspected for four days and then found worthy. From the time of Adam until John the Baptist, Heaven's Lamb was in preparation (2 Pet. 3:8; Jn. 1:29). Jesus is perfect, without sin. Pilate spoke in behalf of all men (Lk. 23:14). There is no fault in Him.

Through Jesus Christ, God has rendered man without excuse (Rom. 2:1). Habakkuk saw the God who became flesh. His vision encompassed Jesus' death and resurrection, a finished work so complete that it lifted the curse from creation. We are overcomers through Him who loved us. Because of our Victor, we are no longer victims.

1 Cor. 10:13, NIV:

*No temptation has seized you except what is common to man. And God is faithful; He will not let you be tempted beyond what you can bear. But when you are tempted, He will also provide a way out so that you can stand up under it.*

So rejoice! It matters not what you see with your natural eyes. There is rest in the day of trouble. Your situation will come to pass, not come to stay. There has no temptation taken you, but such as is common to the God who became man.

Heb. 4:15-16, NIV:

*For we do not have a high priest who is unable to sympathize with our weaknesses, but we have one who has been tempted in every way, just as we are—yet was without sin.*

*Let us then approach the throne of grace with confidence, so that we may receive mercy and find grace to help us in our time of need.*

Messiah would come, born of a virgin. Jesus Christ would walk through the earth, the overcoming Pattern Son. The remainder of Habakkuk's song is a panorama of that glorious procession.

## Chapter Eight

# The Procession

### "Thou didst march through the land"

### Habakkuk 3:4-15

The invisible realm of the Spirit had been opened to Habakkuk. In the first three verses of his song, he extolled the incarnation, the birth of Jesus Christ. Going before us now is the *procession* of God's purpose in coming to earth as a man—from His lowly manger to His glorious triumph over the devil and all the hosts of darkness. Our Lord's life and ministry, from cradle to coronation, now triumphantly passes.

1 John 3:8, KJV:

> *He that committeth sin is of the devil; for the devil sinneth from the beginning. For this purpose the Son of God was manifested, that He might destroy the works of the devil.*

Verses 4-15 of Habakkuk's song magnify Jesus' progressive and complete victory over all enemies as the

Word of God (3:4-6), the Will of God (3:7-9), and the Water of God (3:10-12). The Lord alone can fight America's battles, having won the conflict of the ages (3:13-15).

David, Judah's greatest giant killer, learned the secret of all military strategy. He sat under a simple, single tent (the tabernacle of David) and *sang* to God (2 Sam. 6). Once established in worship, David's authority (throne) was confirmed by the covenant through Nathan the prophet (2 Sam. 7). While the sweet psalmist ministered to the Lord, Jehovah went out and defeated all his enemies (2 Sam. 8). By the time his son Solomon came to power, the victory had been sealed.

1 Kings 5:4, KJV:

> *But now the Lord my God hath given me rest on every side, so that there is neither adversary nor evil occurrent.*

1 Kings 5:4, TLB:

> *"But now," Solomon said to Hiram, "the Lord my God has given Israel peace on every side; I have no foreign enemies or internal rebellions."*

King David was a type of King Jesus, the Champion of the New Testament. The apostle Paul provides a tremendous view of His triumphant *procession* as he compares Jesus Christ to a Roman general returning from the campaigns.

2 Cor. 2:14, KJV:

> *Now thanks be unto God, which always causeth us to triumph in Christ, and maketh manifest the savour of His knowledge by us in every place.*

2 Cor. 2:14, NIV:

*But thanks be to God, who always leads us in triumphal procession in Christ and through us spreads everywhere the fragrance of the knowledge of Him.*

The Greek word for "triumph" that Paul chose is used only here and in Colossians 2:15. It is *thriambĕuŏ* (Strong's #2358) and means "to make an acclamatory procession; to conquer or to give victory." Its root *thrŏĕŏ* means "to clamor; by implication, to frighten." It could be rendered as "to lead in triumph." Picture winning the Super Bowl, or leading a ticker-tape parade ending World War II.

The conquered host's leader would be stripped, shackled, and shamed, then paraded before the multitudes; his spoils: total embarrassment and humiliation. The Roman "captain" (Heb. 2:10) would follow in his chariot, often accompanied by other great warriors. On such occasions, the general's sons, with various officers, rode behind him (Rev. 3:21; 17:14). Then would come the troops in quickstep, shouting, "Triumph! Triumph! Triumph!"

*Strong's Concordance* says that *thriambeuo* is a "noisy iambus," which is a certain meter of verse used in satire. The picture is clear: Jesus defeated the devil. Satan and his crowd seem to be in charge in America, but the day has come for true patriots to arise and enforce the devil's demise.

Let's get noisy! Let's get involved in praise, the activity of the heavens; then we can get effectively involved as concerned citizens in the earth. Praise the Lord! Make a joyful noise! Let's go to the parade! Let's mock the enemy.

His days are shortened in this nation. Jesus whipped him at the cross.

Col. 2:15, KJV:

*And having spoiled principalities and powers, He made a shew of them openly, triumphing over them in it.*

### Jesus, the Light of the World—The Word of God

Habakkuk's song encompasses the whole human family. "God came from Teman," from Edom, Adam, red earth—the stuff from which we all were made (Acts 17:26). In this One who was laid in a manger dwells all the fullness of the Godhead bodily. He houses the Divine nature, the spirit of resurrection life, the name that increased, and became the name to whom everything in Heaven and earth would bow (Is. 9:6-7; Jn. 3:30; Phil. 2:9-11). Habakkuk continues:

Hab. 3:4-6, KJV:

*And His brightness was as the light; He had horns coming out of His hand: and there was the hiding of His power.*

*Before Him went the pestilence, and burning coals went forth at His feet.*

*He stood, and measured the earth: He beheld, and drove asunder the nations; and the everlasting mountains were scattered, the perpetual hills did bow: His ways are everlasting.*

Anyone can complain about how dark it is in America... let's turn on the Light. Throughout the Bible, light represents understanding while darkness speaks of ignorance. God wants to bring this nation out of darkness and into

His marvelous light. Jesus is the Light of the world (Jn. 8:12; 1 John 1:5).

Mt. 5:13-16, KJV:

> *Ye are the salt of the earth: but if the salt have lost his savour, wherewith shall it be salted? it is thenceforth good for nothing, but to be cast out, and to be trodden under foot of men.*
>
> *Ye are the light of the world. A city that is set on an hill cannot be hid.*
>
> *Neither do men light a candle, and put it under a bushel, but on a candlestick; and it giveth light unto all that are in the house.*
>
> *Let your light so shine before men, that they may see your good works, and glorify your Father which is in heaven.*

The Sermon on the Mount is the Constitution of the Kingdom of God. One of the laws that governs God's holy nation is the principle of *influence*. King Jesus explained that the Church is *salt* and *light*, a witness. Radical leftist minorities, 3 percent of the people, cannot continue to railroad the 97 percent who believe in God and decency. We cannot permit godless men to destroy our heritage. We must leaven America and the world with salt and light. We've hidden our influence long enough.

Wake up, America! Arise and shine, Christian friend! Your light has come (Is. 60:1). It's time to be stirred. The night is far spent, the day is at hand. This great nation must cast off the works of darkness and put on the armor of light (Rom. 13:11-14).

Let the triumphant procession begin. Here comes Jesus, the General, the Captain of our salvation. Here comes Jesus, the Light of the world, the Word of God!

Hab. 3:4, KJV:

*And His brightness was as the light; He had horns coming out of His hand: and there was the hiding of His power.*

Hab. 3:4, NIV:

*His splendor was like the sunrise; rays flashed from His hand, where His power was hidden.*

The word that describes the Lord here is "brightness," literally "brilliancy," and comes from a root meaning "to glitter or illuminate." It is translated as "shining" in Proverbs 4:18; Isaiah 4:5; and Habakkuk 3:11. The word for "light" means "illumination; daylight" and is first used in Genesis 1:3. Jesus is the true Light (Jn. 1:9).

Heb. 1:3, KJV:

*Who being the brightness of His glory, and the express image of His person....*

Heb. 1:3, NIV:

*The Son is the radiance of God's glory and the exact representation of His being....*

Heb. 1:3, TLB:

*God's Son shines out with God's glory, and all that God's Son is and does marks Him as God....*

The word for "horns" in Habakkuk 3:4 can mean "a ray of light"; its root is translated as "to shine" (Ex. 34:29-35).

In the Bible, "horns" are figurative for *power*. Jesus Christ is the Horn of salvation raised up for us all (Ps. 132:17; Lk. 1:69). He alone has power to deliver.

This "power" is seen coming forth from the "hand" of the Lord. This could also read, "rays of light are from His side." In the New Testament, God's "hand" is revealed in Ephesians 4:11 to consist of apostles, prophets, evangelists, pastors, and teachers. God's government is Theocratic: God-ruled by those to whom He has delegated His authority. The apostle and prophet especially have been entrusted with the mysteries of His Word (Eph. 2:20; 3:1-5).

All authority centers in Jesus Christ (Mt. 28:18-20). Essentially, no civil or ecclesiastical authority has any authority of its own, but only what has been given by God (Rom. 13:1). Men have abused this authority, but that is about to change.

Habakkuk adds, "And there was the hiding [the concealment] of His power." Men bully and scheme their way into power. The power of the Lord is hidden in His cross (1 Cor. 1:18-24). All great men are true servants. America will become strong again as men learn how to serve one another. Jesus gave Himself for us so that we could learn how to lay down our lives for others. The lowly Carpenter from Nazareth was God in the flesh. The apostles saw the "hiding of His power" and glory on the Mount of Transfiguration.

Mt. 17:1-2, KJV:

> *And after six days Jesus taketh Peter, James, and John his brother, and bringeth them up into an high mountain apart,*

*And was transfigured before them: and His face did shine as the sun, and His raiment was white as the light.*

The word for "power" in Habakkuk 3:4 means "strength (in force, security, majesty, and praise)" and is used 44 times in the Book of Psalms to describe the Lord.

America is in trouble. Our president and people are learning more every day that we cannot solve our problems without the One who is a very present help in time of trouble (Ps. 46:1; 118:14).

Hab. 3:5, KJV:

*Before Him went the pestilence, and burning coals went forth at His feet.*

Hab. 3:5, ASV:

*Before Him went the pestilence, and fiery bolts went forth at His feet.*

This verse amplifies the preceding one as it emphasizes the prowess of the Lord. Verses 3-15 set forth a full display of His glorious might. God had begun to display His power at Sinai (3:3). The "pestilence" here relates to the plagues poured out upon the Egyptians (Ex. 7–12). Following their exodus, the opening of the Red Sea and the Jordan River had brought their deliverance (3:8). Under Joshua's leadership, Jehovah uncovered His bow and subdued the nations of Canaan, even making the sun stand still (3:9-12). Finally, Habakkuk's song returns to the portrayal of Jehovah's triumph over Pharaoh and his army (3:13-15), completing the jubilant procession.

The word for "pestilence" in Habakkuk 3:5 carries the idea of destruction, its root meaning "to subdue." God is rising within His people as He marches across this land. Empowered with the name of Jesus, the Church is a sleeping giant who has begun to rouse. All unrighteousness is going to come under the subjugation of God's Kingdom.

The word for "burning coals" means "a live coal; by analogy, lightning; figuratively, an arrow (as flashing through the air)." For too long the churches of America have been filled with tombstones and not "lively stones" (1 Pet. 2:5). The devil and his army are beginning to feel the heat (Ps. 78:48). This will happen because the Church in America is being found "at His feet." The power of prayer in genuine humility and repentance is turning the tide.

Ruth 3:8, KJV:

*And it came to pass at midnight, that the man was afraid, and turned himself: and, behold, a woman lay at his feet.*

Esther 8:3, KJV:

*And Esther spake yet again before the king, and fell down at his feet, and besought him with tears to put away the mischief of Haman the Agagite, and his device that he had devised against the Jews.*

Ruth and Esther prefigure the New Testament woman, the Church (Eph. 5:22-24). Every Christian in America needs to humble himself before the Lord. We must lay at His feet, not moving till He moves, not speaking till He speaks. Through fasting and prayer, we can thwart the plot of Haman (a type of satan) to destroy God's people.

Hab. 3:6, KJV:

*He stood, and measured the earth: He beheld, and drove asunder the nations; and the everlasting mountains were scattered, the perpetual hills did bow: His ways are everlasting.*

Hab. 3:6, NIV:

*He stood, and shook the earth; He looked, and made the nations tremble. The ancient mountains crumbled and the age-old hills collapsed. His ways are eternal.*

Heb. 12:26-27, KJV:

*Whose voice then shook the earth: but now He hath promised, saying, Yet once more I shake not the earth only, but also heaven.*

*And this word, Yet once more, signifieth the removing of those things that are shaken, as of things that are made, that those things which cannot be shaken may remain.*

The word for "measured" in verse 6 means "to shake." As seen from this passage in Hebrews, Habakkuk 3:4-6 emphasizes the *power* of God's *Word,* the power of Jesus Christ. The Firstborn Son came to earth (3:1-3) with purpose and the power to fulfill it (Rev. 2:26-28).

Here we see the Lord standing (Acts 7:56). The phrase "and measured the earth" is a metaphor of giving victory to Israel in the Old Testament. The Book of Joshua tells the story of Jehovah defeating the enemy and then meting out the land to the twelve tribes. He "drove asunder," or "terrified" heathen nations. So we see the inheritance measured and gained (Ps. 78:55).

He "scattered," or "dashed in pieces" the mountains and hills. There are problems that "loom up" in America that appear to be perpetual. Will things ever be different? Mountains that seem to be "everlasting" are about to be swallowed up by the One who *is* everlasting (Heb. 13:8). Jesus received all authority, then gave it to His people (Mt. 28:18-20). We can change America, but only as we learn the "ways" or the "steps" of the Lord. All must "bow" to Him, the One who is the Word of God.

Phil. 2:10-11, NIV:

*That at the name of Jesus every knee should bow, in heaven and on earth and under the earth,*

*and every tongue confess that Jesus Christ is Lord, to the glory of God the Father.*

## Jesus, the Unveiling of the New Covenant— The Will of God

Hab. 3:7-9, KJV:

*I saw the tents of Cushan in affliction: and the curtains of the land of Midian did tremble.*

*Was the Lord displeased against the rivers? was Thine anger against the rivers? was Thy wrath against the sea, that Thou didst ride upon Thine horses and Thy chariots of salvation?*

*Thy bow was made quite naked, according to the oaths of the tribes, even Thy word. Selah. Thou didst cleave the earth with rivers.*

The song of Habakkuk is a song about Jesus. Its opening stanzas tell of His incarnation (3:1-3) and His incredible power as the *Word* of God (3:4-6). Now we will explore the revelation of the Covenant, which He established with man as the *will* of God (3:7-9). Men will never solve the dilemmas of this nation with mere human wisdom. We must forsake the ways of the flesh and put on the mind of the Spirit.

Hab. 3:7, KJV:

> *I saw the tents of Cushan in affliction: and the curtains of the land of Midian did tremble.*

Hab. 3:7, NIV:

> *I saw the tents of Cushan in distress, the dwellings of Midian in anguish.*

In the days of the judge Gideon (Judg. 6–8), the Midianites and the Amalekites were allies. Amalek was a descendant of Esau and represents the *flesh*. The "tents" of Cushan ("blackness") and the "curtains" of Midian here speak of Jesus' victory over the *flesh*. The word for "affliction" means "to pant, to exert oneself in vain." The word for "tremble" means "to quiver with violent emotion, especially anger or fear." What a description of the futility of men's efforts to heal our nation!

"Midian" means "strife, contention, quarreling (what flesh is all about)." The strife in Washington, the strife in our courts, our churches, our schools, our homes...all strife finds its roots in the human heart. The unveiling of the oath of a New Covenant brought an end to it.

Heb. 6:16, KJV:

*For men verily swear by the greater: and an oath for confirmation is to them an end of all strife.*

Heb. 6:16, NIV:

*Men swear by someone greater than themselves, and the oath confirms what is said and puts an end to all argument.*

Jesus was Heaven's Arbiter; He makes strife shake in its boots. Fully God and fully man, He brought reconciliation by arbitration. Sin had made an impasse between God and man. Fully representing both sides, Jesus' word became law, the law of the Spirit of life (Rom. 8:1-2). God could swear by no greater, so He swore by Himself. He is our Peace (Eph. 2:14). The Prince of Peace became the King of Peace (Is. 9:6-7; Heb. 7:2), the Administrator of Peace. There will never be peace in America's streets until there is peace in the hearts of its people. Then "strife" will be afraid to speak or act.

Hab. 3:8, KJV:

*Was the Lord displeased against the rivers? was Thine anger against the rivers? was Thy wrath against the sea, that Thou didst ride upon Thine horses and Thy chariots of salvation?*

Hab. 3:8, TLB:

*Was it in anger, Lord, You smote the rivers and parted the sea? Were You displeased with them? No, You were sending Your chariots of salvation! All saw*

*Your power! Then springs burst forth upon the earth at
Your command!*

The primary purpose of the Lord's advent is redemptive: He came to deliver, to save His people from the hands of their enemies. "Salvation," the Hebrew term *Yeshua*, is derived from the same root as the name given to Mary's Son, Jesus (Mt. 1:21).

Habakkuk here reminds us of the victories of the Lord at the Red Sea (Ex. 14–15) and the Jordan River (Josh. 3–4). The apostle described Israel's passing through the Red Sea as a picture of the New Covenant truth about water baptism.

1 Cor. 10:1-2, KJV:

*Moreover, brethren, I would not that ye should be
ignorant, how that all our fathers were under the cloud,
and all passed through the sea;*

*And were all baptized unto Moses in the cloud and
in the sea.*

1 Cor. 10:11, KJV:

*Now all these things happened unto them for en-
samples: and they are written for our admonition, upon
whom the ends of the world are come.*

Moses was the mediator of the Old Covenant, Jesus Christ of the New (Jn. 1:17; Gal. 3:19-20; 1 Tim. 2:5). Circumcision was the seal of the Old Covenant, water baptism of the New (Gen. 17; Col. 2:11-12). Just as Pharaoh was cut off at the Red Sea, so satan, the god and prince of this world system, was put under the feet of Jesus. Sin no longer has dominion over us (Rom. 6:1-14). Christian conversion is sealed with water baptism in the name of the Lord, and the power of the enemy is broken. He who believes and is baptized shall be saved (Mk. 16:16).

The Chaldeans invaded Judah; the economy, immorality, and violence are flooding America. The Red Sea is at our backs as these taskmasters thunder down upon us. We feel trapped. There seems to be no way out, but salvation is at hand, within our reach. Our founding fathers entered into a covenant with God. The earliest documents, such as the Mayflower Compact, make it abundantly evident that the first Americans were Christians. As a nation, we must repent and renew covenant with the One who is the Will of God.

Once we make this fresh commitment to God and His Word, He will work with us, not against us, defeating our enemies. In Habakkuk 3:8, His "displeasure" is His "zeal or jealousy"; His "anger" and "wrath," His passion. America has played the whore, courting ungodly ways and means. Our leaders have been seduced away from the Bible and the Constitution. Our Maker and Husband wants to be jealous for this nation again (Is. 54:5).

Ps. 68:1, KJV:

*Let God arise, let His enemies be scattered: let them also that hate Him flee before Him.*

Ps. 68:4, KJV:

*Sing unto God, sing praises to His name: extol Him that rideth upon the heavens by His name JAH, and rejoice before Him.*

Habakkuk then sings about the "chariots of salvation." The psalmist describes the throne-chariot of the Lord going forth in great power. This actually pictures the circuit of the sun from Virgo to Leo (from His virgin birth to His kingship). In the Bible, the sun is the Son and the heavens (astronomy, not astrology) declare His glory (Ps. 8:3; 19:1-6; Mal. 4:2).

The going forth of the chariot also pictures the Ark of the Covenant boldly marching through the wilderness in the days of Moses. The metaphor of the "chariot" has one primary thought: *victory* (2 Kings 6:17). Jesus is not going to win—He won! What can we do? Nothing. Doesn't He need our help? No. We must rest in the day of trouble. How? By letting the Lord teach us how to sing when there is no visible evidence of Him anywhere. We can then sing with Habakkuk as a testimony to real faith.

Whether there is disease in your body, trouble in your marriage, your ministry, your church, your business... everything has to be healed from the inside out. This generation is going to die of old age in the counseling chambers. Each of us must get on the watchtower until he sees the victory of the Lord for himself. Get in His chariot, and He will carry you through!

This "chariot" is found in Song of Solomon 3:6-11 under a different metaphor—a nuptial chariot or marriage litter. In that setting, the Son rides in the place of honor and authority with His Shulamite bride (1 Pet. 3:7). All these thoughts about the chariot portray the triumphal procession of Habakkuk's song. The Lord comes on the chariot of the clouds and the wind. He is the Driver: angry, mighty, resolved in purpose. As with Israel at the

Red Sea, He shows Himself strong against the horse and chariot of this world, the strength of the flesh and those who parade it around. Many famous singers and musicians now pulling the devil's chariot once had their roots in the House of the Lord. They sold the harness of the Lord for a mess of pottage (Gen. 25:29-34).

Hab. 3:9, KJV:

*Thy bow was made quite naked, according to the oaths of the tribes, even Thy word. Selah. Thou didst cleave the earth with rivers.*

Hab. 3:9, NIV:

*You uncovered Your bow, You called for many arrows. Selah. You split the earth with rivers.*

Verse 9 is the key to this part of the song (3:7-9), showing Jesus Christ to be the *unveiling* of the New Covenant. The New Testament is His last *will* and testament. In chapter 1 of this prophecy, Habakkuk learned that he could never know the ways of God with natural understanding. The heart must be awakened by revelation to "see" the Lord (Jn. 3:3; Eph. 1:18).

The last book of the Bible is not the unveiling of the apostle John; it is the Revelation of Jesus Christ. The Greek word for "revelation" is *apŏkalupsis* and means "disclosure; to take off the cover." This is what Habakkuk saw in verse 9. Over two thousand years of religious tradition has still kept most folks in the dark, but that is changing. Religion is useless and cannot help this nation. Our only answer is a blood covenant relationship with God through His Son (Heb. 9:22).

The "bow" in the Bible can speak of a bow and arrow as well as the rainbow (Gen. 9:13-16). In Noah's day, the rainbow was the sign of the *covenant*. In Habakkuk 3:9, the uncovering of the bow is the unveiling of the New Covenant.

Jesus, the Bow of God, was crucified "quite naked." That was done "according to the Word," according to the Scriptures (1 Cor. 15:3-4). A naked bow was also unsheathed until it was finished, until there was no other enemy to conquer, pointing to His "finished" work at Calvary (Ps. 110:1; Jn. 19:30).

The prophet utters "Selah," and pauses a second time. We need to meditate the unsearchable riches of the New Testament in His blood. Habakkuk, along with all the other Old Testament prophets, diligently inquired of these things, and foretold the grace that would come to us (1 Pet. 1:10-11). We can now search out a more sure word of prophecy.

This second "selah" reveals our spiritual youth in God (1 John 2:12-14). The Feast of Weeks, the Feast of Pentecost, was in the third month, the same time that the Law was given at Sinai (Ex. 19:1; Lev. 23:15-16). Although speaking with other tongues is the historic and experiential Pentecostal distinctive, a true Pentecost happens when the law of the unveiled New Covenant is written upon our hearts. Men today can be filled with the Holy Spirit just as the early Church in the Book of Acts. Selah...

The word for "oaths" in Habakkuk 3:9 means "something sworn." Jesus Christ was made the Son by oath, by covenant (Rom. 1:1-4; Heb. 6:16-20; Heb. 7:20-21, 28). The root word for "oath" is *sheba'* and means "seven," the

Bible number denoting completeness and perfection. Jesus' finished work on the cross was the complete provision for the needs of America and the world.

Rom. 8:29, KJV:

*For whom He did foreknow, He also did predestinate to be conformed to the image of His Son, that He might be the firstborn among many brethren.*

Habakkuk's song recollects the words of Deuteronomy 32:40-42. In the time of Moses, weapons of war were sworn into service. The Messiah was appointed from eternity (Acts 2:23; 4:28). God has also sworn into His service His "arrows," the instruments of war needed for the battle long before it is actually fought. These are the "brethren" of whom Paul speaks. The Father uncovered the Bow and then called for many arrows: men and women whom He can direct. As arrows of the Lord, we are joined to the Bow in covenant, pulled back by the hand (Eph. 4:11), and sent forth with purpose (tension and energy). The "arrows" of the Lord are the sons of God in the image of the Firstborn (Ps. 18:14; 77:17; Zech. 9:14).

When Jesus died on the cross, He did "cleave the earth." He rent, literally "split or severed," the veil, ripping it from the top to the bottom (Mt. 27:51; Eph. 2:14-16). The word for "cleave" in verse 9 means "to rend, break, rip, or open." All that had been hidden from ages and generations was now made manifest. The New Covenant, the will of God, the image of the invisible God, was unveiled.

Col. 1:26-27, TLB:

*He has kept this secret for centuries and*

*generations past, but now at last it has pleased Him to tell it to those who love Him and live for Him, and the riches and glory of His plan are for you Gentiles, too. And this is the secret: Christ in your hearts is your only hope of glory.*

### Jesus, the River of the Spirit—The Water of God

Hab. 3:10-12, KJV:

*The mountains saw Thee, and they trembled: the over-flowing of the water passed by: the deep uttered his voice, and lifted up his hands on high.*

*The sun and moon stood still in their habitation: at the light of Thine arrows they went, and at the shining of Thy glittering spear.*

*Thou didst march through the land in indignation, Thou didst thresh the heathen in anger.*

As Habakkuk's song unfolds, it tells the old, old story of Jesus and His love. The Word was made flesh (3:1-3). We have seen the power of His *Word* (3:4-6) and the unveiling of His Testament or *Will* (3:7-9); having believed and been baptized (Mk. 16:16), we now meet Him who is the *Water* of God (Jn. 7:38), the River of the Holy Spirit.

The prophet does this by describing a cloudburst, very much like that of Psalm 77:17-20. The end of verse 9 could read, "Thou didst cleave the earth into rivers." God's purpose is clear: to water the earth, to send His Word and His Spirit to the nations. We are to be saved, baptized in water, and filled with the Holy Ghost (Hab. 3:3,8,10; Acts 2:38; 1 John 5:8).

Hab. 3:10, KJV:

*The mountains saw Thee, and they trembled: the
overflowing of the water passed by: the deep uttered his
voice, and lifted up his hands on high.*

Hab. 3:10, NIV:

*The mountains saw You and writhed. Torrents of water
swept by; the deep roared and lifted its waves on high.*

Hab. 3:10, TLB:

*The mountains watched and trembled. Onward swept
the raging water. The mighty deep cried out, announcing its surrender to the Lord.*

America must return to Jesus, the One who baptizes
with the Holy Ghost and fire. The might and power of
men cannot compare with the power of the Spirit (Zech.
4:6; Mt. 3:11). The "mountains," the kingdoms that men
have built, "tremble," or "writhe in pain" as America begins to fear the Lord. This word is especially used to describe birth pangs. This nation is travailing now.

Mt. 24:8, KJV:

*All these are the beginning of sorrows.*

Mt. 24:8, NIV:

*All these are the beginning of birth pains.*

Man-made religion hates these truths about the Holy
Ghost, but the way of the Lord is the way of His Spirit (Rom. 8:14). The "overflowing of the water" that Habakkuk saw is the Pentecostal experience, the Holy Ghost

baptism. An unprecedented outpouring of the Holy Spirit throughout the nations is bringing tremors and earthquakes to every political and denominational system.

Gen. 7:11, KJV:

*In the six hundredth year of Noah's life, in the second month, the seventeenth day of the month, the same day were all the fountains of the great deep broken up, and the windows of heaven were opened.*

Jn. 7:38, KJV:

*He that believeth on Me, as the scripture hath said, out of his belly shall flow rivers of living water.*

Jn. 16:13, KJV:

*Howbeit when He, the Spirit of truth, is come, He will guide you into all truth: for He shall not speak of Himself; but whatsoever He shall hear, that shall He speak: and He will shew you things to come.*

Acts 1:5, KJV:

*For John truly baptized with water; but ye shall be baptized with the Holy Ghost not many days hence.*

Eph. 5:17-18, KJV:

*Wherefore be ye not unwise, but understanding what the will of the Lord is.*

*And be not drunk with wine, wherein is excess; but be filled with the Spirit.*

The word for "overflowing" in Habakkuk 3:10 means "a gush of water," and is also translated as "flood, shower, storm, tempest." The Hebrew word for "passed by" speaks of any kind of transition. There was a time in America when 20-minute sermonettes for Christianettes once a week was enough "church." Our only hope for survival in the 90s is to be filled with the Holy Ghost until (like the Church of the Book of Acts) we live daily by His supernatural power (see Mk. 16:15-20; Acts 1:8; 2:22; 3:12; 4:7,33; 6:8; 8:10,13; 10:38; 19:11).

We must make that transition. This is happening in churches all over America, regardless of denomination. Hungry pastors and people are beginning to pray and ask the Lord to fill them and their local church with the Holy Spirit. It's not up for debate any more. A man with an experience is never at the mercy of a man with an argument (Ps. 34:8; 1 John 1:1-4). The same power that raised Jesus Christ from the dead is being poured out upon our land.

Rom. 8:11, KJV:

*But if the Spirit of Him that raised up Jesus from the dead dwell in you, He that raised up Christ from the dead shall also quicken your mortal bodies by His Spirit that dwelleth in you.*

Acts 2:4, KJV:

*And they were all filled with the Holy Ghost, and began to speak with other tongues, as the Spirit gave them utterance.*

What happens when a person is filled with the Holy Spirit? Habakkuk describes it for us in verse 10. The deep "utters" or "gives" its voice. This happened upon each of the five occasions in the Book of Acts when the early Church received the infilling of the Holy Spirit (see Acts 2:4; 8:18,21; 9:17 with 1 Cor. 14:18; Acts 10:46; 19:6).

Hyper-dispensationalists treat the Book of Acts like a separate age. Their theory conveniently excuses the evident void of God's supernatural power in their midst. They need to understand that these things happened only the day before yesterday (1 Pet. 3:8). Then and now, a Spirit-filled man is not ashamed or embarrassed to "lift up his hands on high" (see Neh. 8:6; Ps. 28:2; 63:4; 119:48; 134:2; 141:2; Lam. 2:19; 3:41; 1 Tim. 2:8; Heb. 12:12). America must cry, announcing its surrender to the One who baptizes with the Holy Ghost and fire.

Hab. 3:11, KJV:

*The sun and moon stood still in their habitation: at the light of Thine arrows they went, and at the shining of Thy glittering spear.*

Hab. 3:11, TLB:

*The lofty sun and moon began to fade, obscured by brilliance from Your arrows and the flashing of Your glittering spear.*

The Pentecostal baptism is the key of David (Rev. 3:7), unlocking the heavenlies, the supernatural realm of the Spirit. The miracle described in verse 11 actually happened in the tenth chapter of the Book of Joshua as well as at the crucifixion (Mt. 27:45; Lk. 23:45; compare Is. 60:19). Once again, God is intervening in the affairs of the nations.

When the real Sun "stood still" in Matthew 20:32-34, He opened the eyes of men who were blind. Once America opens its heart to the reality of the power of the Holy Spirit, Jesus will have compassion on us and touch the eyes of our understanding (Eph. 1:18). Then we will follow Him, as the loftiness of our natural understanding fades, obscured by His brilliance. Until then, the blind will continue to lead the blind (Mt. 15:14). The problem is, the ditch is almost full.

As noted in verse 9, the Lord's "arrows," literally "thunderbolts," and His "glittering (gleaming, flashing) spear" are His sons, His people. We are to be His arrows from the bow, His sword from the sheath, His hand extended, branching out from Him who is the true Vine (Jn. 15:1-5). We are to be lightning, obeying Him in a flash, going forth to do His will. Like spiritual laser beams, we are being sent forth to heal the nations. We are a people of light, a people of the Word (Ps. 119:105; Heb. 4:12).

The Holy Spirit is emphasized in verse 10; the Word of God, the Light, in verse 11 (Prov. 1:23).

The word for "light" in Habakkuk 3:11 means "illumination or luminary." The word "shining" means "brilliancy" and "to glitter," and could be translated as "lightning." Up till now, the world has smothered real Christians. But we are shaking ourselves to arise as the Light of the world. We are becoming aggressive in the might and power of the Lord. Darkness will never come to the Light, lest its deeds be reproved. We must abandon our comfort zones to address the darkness. The only battles that the devil has won in America are those in which the Church did not engage him.

Hab. 3:12, KJV:

*Thou didst march through the land in indignation,
Thou didst thresh the heathen in anger.*

Hab. 3:12, NIV:

*In wrath You strode through the earth and in anger
You threshed the nations.*

"Thou didst march through the land…"

The prophet sums up this section by telling us again what the Lord did when He came from Teman (3:3). As a man, Jesus defeated the devil. He threshed the "heathen" in anger, overcoming death, hell, and the grave. Then He ascended, passing through the heavens on the way to His coronation (Heb. 4:14-16; Ps. 15 and 24). This word for "march" means "to pace; step regularly; to mount upward." Jesus strode through the earth, defeating sin, sickness, poverty, and death (Acts 10:38). Then He mounted upward, passing through the heavens to ascend the throne.

There is nothing in this earth, no "heathen" spouse, boss, politician, or preacher, that you cannot overcome in the name of Jesus. No "heathen" person or thing can rob you of your joy unless you allow it. The only thing that has power over you is your own tongue. Stop making excuses like the man by the pool (Jn. 5:1-7). "I'd get in the water, Lord, but somebody is always getting in my way. Besides, no one will help me." No! Jesus' victory renders us without excuse. We must follow the Lamb.

Ps. 37:23, KJV:

*The steps of a good man are ordered by the Lord: and
He delighteth in his way.*

1 Pet. 2:21, NIV:

*To this you were called, because Christ suffered for you, leaving you an example, that you should follow in His steps.*

The glorious Church, the Army of the Lord, is following their Captain. Having been delivered by the blood, the water, and the Spirit (Hab. 3:3,8,10; 1 John 5:8), we are marching through America, fulfilling the Great Commission (Mt. 28:18-20; Mk. 16:15-20; Acts 1:8). The God who is in us now works with us and through us.

The word for "anger" in Habakkuk 3:12 is the same as verse 8, speaking of the Lord's "passion." It describes His avenging wrath. Majestically, the Lord marches through America on a corrective expedition, to expose and discipline those opposing His Church (Is. 63:1-6). Once again, Jesus is cleansing the temple.

The word for "indignation" in verse 12 has the thought of the Lord's anger "boiling up." There are a lot of things that are cooking in this nation. The pot is boiling and the fire is hot. Jehovah is about to serve up His righteous judgments. He has begun to "thresh" or "trample" the "heathen," those who, like Jehoiakim of old, mock the Bible and the One who wrote it. Jesus has already put the devil under His feet (Eph. 1:20-23). His Church now arises to finish what He began.

Rom. 16:20, KJV:

*And the God of peace shall bruise Satan under your feet shortly. The grace of our Lord Jesus Christ be with you. Amen.*

### Jesus, the Victor Over the Kingdom of Darkness— God Wins!

Hab. 3:13-15, KJV:

*Thou wentest forth for the salvation of Thy people, even for salvation with Thine anointed; Thou woundedst the head out of the house of the wicked, by discovering the foundation unto the neck. Selah.*

*Thou didst strike through with his staves the head of his villages: they came out as a whirlwind to scatter me: their rejoicing was as to devour the poor secretly.*

*Thou didst walk through the sea with Thine horses, through the heap of great waters.*

Jesus Christ is the *Word*, the *Will*, and the *Water* of God. Now we see that in the battle of the ages, He was the *Winner*! The prophet completes this part of the song by returning to the Old Testament imagery of Israel's deliverance from Pharaoh and their bondage in Egypt. Contained in these three verses is the account of the Messiah's complete victory over satan and all the hosts of darkness. God wins!

Hab. 3:13, KJV:

*Thou wentest forth for the salvation of Thy people, even for salvation with Thine anointed; Thou woundedst the head out of the house of the wicked, by discovering the foundation unto the neck. Selah.*

Hab. 3:13, NIV:

*You came out to deliver Your people, to save Your anointed one. You crushed the leader of the land of wickedness, You stripped him from head to foot. Selah.*

Hab. 3:13, Ferrar Fenton:

*You came to save Your people; with Your Messiah to win; crushed the chief of the house of rebellion, trod on the base of his neck!*

"Thine anointed" refers to King David and then to the Heavenly David, Jesus Christ the Messiah (2 Chron. 6:42). As noted, the very name "Jesus" means "salvation," literally "liberty, deliverance, and prosperity." These are words that are meant to describe our nation and its people. Let us embrace the Savior, the One who went forth from the bosom of the Father as the Lord's "anointed," His Messianic title, especially in the Book of Psalms (see Ps. 2:2; 18:50; 20:6; 28:8; 84:9; 89:38, 51; and 132:10).

Gen. 3:15, NIV:

*And I will put enmity between you and the woman, and between your offspring and hers; he will crush your head, and you will strike his heel.*

Jesus, the Seed of the woman, "wounded" the serpent's head and "crushed the leader of the land of wickedness." The word Habakkuk used for "woundedst" is a primitive root meaning "to dash asunder; to crush, smash or violently plunge; to subdue or destroy." This word is used in Judges 5:26 to describe the victory of the woman Jael over the evil Sisera when she "pierced" his temples with the "nail." Jesus is that Nail in a sure place, the Word of God (see Eccles. 12:11; Ezra 9:8; Is. 22:23-25; Zech. 10:4). As Christians, we don't have to take a back seat to the devil and his followers. Let's put the Bible and prayer back into our homes, churches, and schools. Let's pierce him all the way through.

Gen. 3:15, NKJ:

> *And I will put enmity between you and the woman, and between your seed and her Seed; He shall bruise your head, and you shall bruise His heel.*

The Hebrew word for "bruise" in this first promise of the coming Messiah means "to gape; to snap at; overwhelm." To "gape" is to open the mouth wide. The Father is a thinker. The Thinker thought and then the Thinker spoke, opened His mouth wide, and the Word was made flesh.

The warfare between God's Anointed and satan's kingdom of sin culminated in the great battle on Golgotha, which ended in satan's complete and everlasting defeat. There the head of the house of the wicked received his mortal wound, "overwhelmed" by the love of God (Jn. 3:16). The foundation of his house was revealed as falsehood and sinking sand; its walls as fraud and deception; its interior as chambers of iniquity inhabited by the dead.

The word "house" in Habakkuk 3:13 refers to the realm or kingdom of darkness. Jesus took the roof off that house when He bruised the serpent's "head." Such a house can no longer protect its inhabitants against wind and weather. The picture here is a house struck by lightning in a fierce storm. The roof and foundation are gone and the walls demolished; then it's gutted by fire.

America is filled with wickedness. Jesus has already dealt with the "wicked" one. This word in verse 13 speaks of that which is "morally wrong; to disturb or violate." Men deal with the body and the soul, or the mind. Here's where the psychics and the self-help humanists have to leave the ball game. Only God can change the spirit, the heart of man. The basic cause, the "foundation," of America's ills is in the heart.

The root word for "foundation" here means "to set; to found; to sit down together, to settle or consult." Satan has devised his strategies in the gates of hell, but he is a defeated foe. We are not to be ignorant of his "devices," his thoughts. Jesus has "discovered" or "made bare" every devilish scheme to destroy this great nation, having stood on his neck, stripping him from head to foot (see Josh. 10:24-25; Ps. 2:1-6; Amos 9:1; 2 Thess. 2:8).

Mt. 16:18, KJV:

*And I say also unto thee, That thou art Peter, and upon this rock I will build My church; and the gates of hell shall not prevail against it.*

2 Cor. 2:11, KJV:

*Lest Satan should get an advantage of us: for we are not ignorant of his devices.*

The prophet then utters his third and final "selah," pausing to consider the once-and-for-all eternal triumph of the Lord Jesus over all enemies. This points ahead to the time when the mature, glorious Church will also put all enemies under her feet. This third "selah" reveals a people of the Most Holy Place in the Feast of Tabernacles.

Habakkuk's sob became a song when he saw that Jesus would come and defeat the devil and all his demons. The One about whom the prophet sang was exalted far above all principalities and powers (Eph. 1:20-23; 6:12).

Hab. 3:14, KJV:

*Thou didst strike through with his staves the head of his villages: they came out as a whirlwind to scatter me: their rejoicing was as to devour the poor secretly.*

Hab. 3:14, NIV:

*With his own spear You pierced his head when his warriors stormed out to scatter us, gloating as though about to devour the wretched who were in hiding.*

Habakkuk identifies himself with Israel in this verse and depicts the treatment God offers the invaders of His land. By mutual destruction (see Judg. 7:22; 1 Sam. 14:20; 2 Chron. 22-24), the enemy will fall by their own weapons.

David slew the champion Goliath; then the army of Israel slew the rest of the Philistines. Jesus defeated the devil; then He dealt with every principality and power. He did "strike through" them on the cross; this word means "to puncture; to perforate with violence; to pierce (with holes)." What prophecy! Our Lord's hands, feet, and side were struck through that awful day.

The word for "staves" in verse 14 means "a branch (as extending); a tribe (3:9); a rod or staff." Jesus the Vine defeated the devil; now His army, His branches, complete the demise of every demon.

In the Tabernacle of Moses, a divine pattern (Ex. 25:40) of Jesus and the Church, there were four pieces of furniture that were carried with "staves." These are our weapons:

1. *The Brazen Altar–the cross.*
2. *The Table of Shewbread–the Word of God.*
3. *The Golden Altar of Incense–intercession.*
4. *The Ark of the Covenant–His lordship.*

Ps. 110:5-6, KJV:

*The Lord at Thy right hand shall strike through kings in the day of His wrath.*

*He shall judge among the heathen, He shall fill the places with the dead bodies; He shall wound the heads over many countries.*

Eph. 6:12, NIV:

*For our struggle is not against flesh and blood, but against the rulers, against the authorities, against the powers of this dark world and against the spiritual forces of evil in the heavenly realms.*

Col. 2:15, NIV:

*And having disarmed the powers and authorities, He made a public spectacle of them, triumphing over them by the cross.*

1 John 3:8, NIV:

*He who does what is sinful is of the devil, because the devil has been sinning from the beginning. The reason the Son of God appeared was to destroy the devil's work.*

Jesus defeated the devil and then dismantled his kingdom. Jesus struck through the head of the "villages," literally "chieftains." Our Captain spoiled and disarmed principalities and powers, triumphing over them in His cross. In America, these "chieftains" dominate the kingdoms of sports, movies, music, and mammon. These villagers are the inhabitants of unfenced cities or the open country; they live in the hearts of the lawless. The Church now arises to enforce the law, to occupy the territory that Jesus recovered (1 Sam. 30:18-20; Lk. 19:13).

Since the new administration took office, these demons have come out like a "whirlwind" upon the people of America. This word means "to rush upon or to toss." Their purpose is to "scatter" or "dash in pieces" the righteous. Especially through the economy, their "rejoicing" or "exultation" is to "devour" the "poor" or "depressed" secretly (1 Pet. 5:8). Their motive is bad enough, but their method is underhanded. The word for "secretly" means "a concealer, a covert; to hide by covering." Every cover-up will be shouted from the housetops in the Day of the Lord. The lid is coming off everything. The enemy will be exposed and defeated in every area of American life.

Hab. 3:15, KJV:

> *Thou didst walk through the sea with Thine horses, through the heap of great waters.*

Hab. 3:15, TLB:

> *Your horsemen marched across the sea; the mighty waters piled high.*

This part of the song (3:13-15) is summed up in the victory of the Lord. Israel "marched across the sea" and walked dry-shod over the Jordan River when "the mighty waters piled high" (Ex. 14–15; Josh. 3–4).

The *procession* has ended. The King now sits enthroned, triumphant over all His enemies!

This was good news for the prophet. If God wrought so wondrously in bringing His people out of Egypt, could He not do it again to bring them out of the captivity of Babylon? There is no limitation to His power, and His mercy is past finding out. Habakkuk had climbed the mountain of faith and trust, but was yet to reach the pinnacle.

The word for "walk" in verse 15 means "to tread, to walk; to string a bow (by treading on it in bending)." Compare the "bow" of Habakkuk 3:9. The word for "heap" means "to bubble or boil up." The Lord shall ride through the heap of great waters, through the wildest and stormiest waves of persecution and bloodshed threatening to overwhelm and swallow His people (Is. 54:17; Ps. 46). But the Church triumphant is alive and well!

Get ready, America! the Lord is stirring Himself within the midst of His people. Habakkuk, the prophetic Church, has seen the Lord. We have learned how to rest in the day of trouble.

# Chapter Nine

# The Peace

## "Rest in the day of trouble"

## Habakkuk 3:16-18

The Theophany had come and gone. The heavens had opened to reveal the vision of the Lord. To the natural eye, the land of Judah was still filled with idolatry; the Chaldeans were still at the door. But faith had brought hope. Habakkuk was at rest in the day of trouble. He had seen the One who was his *Peace.*

Hab. 3:16-18, KJV:

> *When I heard, my belly trembled; my lips quivered at the voice: rottenness entered into my bones, and I trembled in myself, that I might rest in the day of trouble: when he cometh up unto the people, he will invade them with his troops.*
>
> *Although the fig tree shall not blossom, neither shall fruit be in the vines; the labour of the olive shall fail, and the fields shall yield no meat; the flock shall be cut off from the fold, and there shall be no herd in the stalls:*

> *Yet I will rejoice in the Lord, I will joy in the God of my salvation.*

These closing verses show Christ dwelling in the heart by faith (Eph. 3:17), especially in a time when there is no visible evidence of His presence. This peace is manifested as the fivefold triumph of faith (2 Cor. 5:7):

1. *We rest in God, regardless.*
2. *We joy in every circumstance.*
3. *We are strong for ourselves and then support others.*
4. *We walk by faith and not by sight.*
5. *We sing continually unto the Lord.*

This abundant living is the "bait" the Church will use to hook the nations. Peace, joy, faith, hope...are to be found only in the presence of the Lord.

Hab. 3:16, KJV:

> *When I heard, my belly trembled; my lips quivered at the voice: rottenness entered into my bones, and I trembled in myself, that I might rest in the day of trouble: when he cometh up unto the people, he will invade them with his troops.*

Hab. 3:16, AMP:

> *I heard, and my (whole inner self) trembled, my lips quivered at the sound. Rottenness enters my bones and under me—down to my feet—I tremble. I will wait quietly for the day of trouble and distress, when there shall come up against (my) people him who is about to invade and oppress them.*

Habakkuk had been struck in the core of his being. He had "heard" the living Word (Hab. 3:2) in his "belly," the Hebrew word for "womb." Like the patriarch Jacob (Gen. 32:25), the prophet had been smitten in the thigh, the place of strength and reproduction. God has hit America in the gut...hard. He has our attention now. Our creative genius hasn't produced any real answers...in fact, we're not even sure about the questions (1 Kings 10:1-3).

Habakkuk "trembled" and "quivered with violent emotion." He had actually seen the Lord. Many have abused the prophetic ministry, and novices are quick on the trigger to say, "Thus saith the Lord!" But when a man really hears God's "voice," his lips will "quiver." This word means "vibration; to rattle together (as the teeth chattering with fear)." Real revelation will break your heart. Then you will repent and change.

Prov. 12:4, KJV:

*A virtuous woman is a crown to her husband: but she that maketh ashamed is as rottenness in his bones.*

Prov. 14:30, KJV:

*A sound heart is the life of the flesh: but envy the rottenness of the bones.*

The prophet experienced the fear of the Lord. When "rottenness" entered Habakkuk's bones, he felt two emotions: shame and envy. He was ashamed that he had been trapped in the lower realms of "how long" and "why," and he envied those who would live in the New Covenant day when his "vision" would be fulfilled. Beholding

Jesus' life and ministry was enough to turn Habakkuk's sob into a song. The prophet of faith was at peace, though Nebuchadnezzar was about to ascend Jerusalem and "invade" or "attack" with his troops.

What Habakkuk saw and heard impacted his "bones." The bones form the structure of the body. These "bones" can picture the framework of America's idolatry, individually and collectively. If there is a conspiracy, it will crumble and its "bones" will rot. The Lord has begun to take away everything that He did not tell us to do. The arrangement and design of the way we think and act in America, the "bones" of our philosophies that are not in agreement with the Bible—everything is dealt with in the Day of the Lord. We are going to feel it "down to the feet" as the wind of His Spirit levels everything back down to the foundation!

Zech. 9:12, NIV:

*Return to your fortress, O prisoners of hope; even now I announce that I will restore twice as much to you.*

Lk. 24:21, NIV:

*But we had hoped that He was the one who was going to redeem Israel. And what is more, it is the third day since all this took place.*

2 Pet. 1:20, KJV:

*Knowing this first, that no prophecy of the scripture is of any private interpretation.*

The stronghold, the fortress, is the Lord Himself. He is our Rock, and we are secure in Christ. The Lord has predetermined our glorious destiny, but we persist in our own interpretation of His expectation. Like Cleopas and his friend on the Emmaus road, we must understand that the redemption that He brought and the Israel that He came to redeem is bigger than we thought. They had a Jewish tradition, a human expectation, a "how long" and a "why."

Lk. 24:25-27, NIV:

> *He said to them, "How foolish you are, and how slow of heart to believe all that the prophets have spoken!*
>
> *"Did not the Christ have to suffer these things and then enter His glory?"*
>
> *And beginning with Moses and all the Prophets, He explained to them what was said in all the Scriptures concerning Himself.*

All of us in America are facing things that we did not anticipate. It doesn't agree with the way we want to live. We don't like it. God is going to let us wallow around in it for a while, maybe the rest of Clinton's administration. What can we do? Nothing but get on the watchtower and let God interpret Himself. His is the only sensible explanation.

"...that I might 'rest' in the day of trouble..."

We have come to the phrase that inspired this writing. Like Habakkuk, we can "rest" in the day of trouble! There is hope for America.

The word for "rest" in verse 16 is *nûwach* (Strong's #5117) and means "to rest; settle down." *Vine's Dictionary* adds, "remain; be quiet." There is a righteous remnant in this nation who have learned how to "rest." This word reveals God's blessings upon His covenant people, and is used about 65 times in the Old Testament, including:

Gen. 8:4, KJV:

*And the ark rested in the seventh month, on the seventeenth day of the month, upon the mountains of Ararat.*

Ex. 20:11, KJV:

*For in six days the Lord made heaven and earth, the sea, and all that in them is, and rested the seventh day: wherefore the Lord blessed the sabbath day, and hallowed it.*

Ex. 33:14, KJV:

*And He said, My presence shall go with thee, and I will give thee rest.*

Num. 11:25, KJV:

*And the Lord came down in a cloud, and spake unto him, and took of the spirit that was upon him, and gave it unto the seventy elders: and it came to pass, that, when the spirit rested upon them, they prophesied, and did not cease.*

1 Kings 5:4, KJV:

*But now the Lord my God hath given me rest on every side, so that there is neither adversary nor evil occurrent.*

Is. 28:12, KJV:

*To whom He said, This is the rest wherewith ye may cause the weary to rest; and this is the refreshing: yet they would not hear.*

"...that I might rest in the day of 'trouble'..."

Economically, morally, spiritually...things are really getting "tight" in America and the nations.

The word for "trouble" in Habakkuk 3:16 is the Hebrew word *tsârâh* (Strong's #6869), which means "tightness." It is rendered as "adversary, adversity, affliction, anguish, distress, tribulation, and trouble" in the King James Version. It is taken from another word meaning "narrow; a tight place (trouble); an opponent (as crowding); to cramp." *Vine's Dictionary* translates *tsârâh* as "straits, or distress (in a psychological or spiritual sense)." It is used in the following verses:

Gen. 35:3, KJV:

*And let us arise, and go up to Bethel; and I will make there an altar unto God, who answered me in the day of my distress, and was with me in the way which I went.*

Job 5:19, KJV:

*He shall deliver thee in six troubles: yea, in seven there shall no evil touch thee.*

Ps. 91:15, KJV:

*He shall call upon Me, and I will answer him: I will be with him in trouble; I will deliver him, and honour him.*

Prov. 17:17, KJV:

*A friend loveth at all times, and a brother is born for adversity.*

Jer. 30:7, KJV:

*Alas! for that day is great, so that none is like it: it is even the time of Jacob's trouble; but he shall be saved out of it.*

Dan. 12:1, KJV:

*And at that time shall Michael stand up, the great prince which standeth for the children of thy people: and there shall be a time of trouble, such as never was since there was a nation even to that same time: and at that time thy people shall be delivered, every one that shall be found written in the book.*

The "day of trouble" is mentioned several other times in the Bible. Christians need not fear, for our names are written in the Lamb's book of life. God is our refuge and strength, a very present help in trouble. As He revealed Himself to Habakkuk and others, He will answer us in the day of our distress.

2 Kings 19:3, KJV:

*And they said unto him, Thus saith Hezekiah, This day is a day of trouble, and of rebuke, and blasphemy: for the children are come to the birth, and there is not strength to bring forth.*

Ps. 20:1, KJV:

*The Lord hear thee in the day of trouble; the name of the God of Jacob defend thee.*

Nahum 1:7, KJV:

*The Lord is good, a strong hold in the day of trouble; and He knoweth them that trust in Him.*

Zeph. 1:15, KJV:

*That day is a day of wrath, a day of trouble and distress, a day of wasteness and desolation, a day of darkness and gloominess, a day of clouds and thick darkness.*

## God, Where Are You?

In the 60s, liberal theologians invented a new doctrine, proclaiming, "God is dead!" The basis for their nonsense was a humanistic worldview. "We have looked into society, into our world, even into our churches, and we don't see God anywhere. Therefore, He is dead." Thus was their logic and reasoning.

The verse before us is a synopsis of Habakkuk's original sob. It is the theme of the Book of Ecclesiastes, the "Book of the Natural Man" who views all things from "under the sun." God is nowhere to be found. You can't see Him, hear Him, or feel Him; He isn't anywhere in what you are praying about. All is vanity and vexation of spirit.

In one verse, Habakkuk now describes the blight and barrenness of his beloved nation, a portent of what is taking place in America and the Church today.

Hab. 3:17, KJV:

*Although the fig tree shall not blossom, neither shall fruit be in the vines; the labour of the olive shall fail, and the fields shall yield no meat; the flock shall be cut off from the fold, and there shall be no herd in the stalls.*

Hab. 3:17, TLB:

*Even though the fig trees are all destroyed, and there is neither blossom left nor fruit; though the olive crops all fail, and the fields lie barren; even if the flocks die in the fields and the cattle barns are empty.*

This verse describes the very life's blood of the nation; without the fig and olive trees, without the sheep and cattle, Judah could not exist. Those great Christian virtues and values which built America are nowhere to be seen. Here is a picture of the dearth upon the Church and our nation, revealing the principle of no fruit, food, or flocks in three dimensions: spirit, soul, and body (1 Thess. 5:23).

1. *Spiritual condition–spirit realm.*
2. *Emotional condition–soul realm.*
3. *Physical condition–body or natural realm.*
4. *Financial condition–body or natural realm.*
5. *Domestic condition–body or natural realm.*

The "fig tree," a symbol of security and hope, represents the nation of Judah as a whole. The blooms of the fig tree always appear before the leaves in spring. To "blossom" means "to break forth as a bud, bloom; to spread; to flourish." This word is used in Numbers 17:5 to designate God's chosen priesthood and in Psalms 72:7; 92:12-13; and Proverbs 11:28 to describe the "flourishing" of the righteous. As seen in Chapter Two of this writing, there is a growing unrighteousness in America. We need a priestly people to step forward who know how to pray, worship, and show mercy. As in the days of Ezra the scribe, we need ministry with the mind of Christ.

Ezra 2:62-63, KJV:

*These sought their register among those that were reckoned by genealogy, but they were not found: therefore were they, as polluted, put from the priesthood.*

*And the Tirshatha said unto them, that they should not eat of the most holy things, till there stood up a priest with Urim and with Thummim.*

The word for "fruit" in Habakkuk 3:17 means "produce; crop or wealth" and is taken from a root meaning "to flow; to bring (especially with pomp)." This portrays the natural and spiritual wealth of Judah and America. The economic and spiritual indicators show that we are hurting in both areas. American-made products have decreased in quality. Our spiritual fruit, godly character, is no longer pleasing to the Lord. Many great churches and preachers once flowed with the Spirit; now, by their traditions they have nullified the Word (Mk. 7:13). We have nothing to bring to the Lord.

Deut. 16:16, KJV:

*Three times in a year shall all thy males appear before the Lord thy God in the place which He shall choose; in the feast of unleavened bread, and in the feast of weeks, and in the feast of tabernacles: and they shall not appear before the Lord empty.*

Emblematic of the nation (Deut. 8:8), the "olive" tree was a symbol of vigor, strength, and prosperity; its most important product, the illuminating oil (the best oil being obtained from the green olive fruit). Oil, of course, is a symbol for the Holy Spirit, as seen in Exodus 27:20; 30:24; and Zechariah 4:12, as well as these:

1 Sam 16:13, KJV:

*Then Samuel took the horn of oil, and anointed him in the midst of his brethren: and the Spirit of the Lord*

*came upon David from that day forward. So Samuel
rose up, and went to Ramah.*

Ps. 23:5, KJV:

*Thou preparest a table before me in the presence of
mine enemies: Thou anointest my head with oil; my cup
runneth over.*

Ps. 45:7, KJV:

*Thou lovest righteousness, and hatest wickedness:
therefore God, thy God, hath anointed thee with the oil
of gladness above thy fellows.*

Is. 61:3, KJV:

*To appoint unto them that mourn in Zion, to give
unto them beauty for ashes, the oil of joy for mourning,
the garment of praise for the spirit of heaviness; that
they might be called trees of righteousness, the planting
of the Lord, that He might be glorified.*

The Church in America has replaced the anointing of
the Holy Spirit with lifeless programs and meaningless
agendas. But none of that has broken the yoke, the
problems that bind our land and its people (Is. 10:27). The
"labour," literally the "action or activity" of the anointing,
has failed. We have oiled political and religious machinery with everything except Holy Ghost living and praying. The Ark of the Covenant, the glory of the Lord, has
"departed," literally been "denuded (in a disgraceful
sense), exiled, stripped" (see Gen. 9:21; 2 Kings 17:23; Jer.
49:10; Nahum 3:5).

1 Sam. 4:21-22, KJV:

*And she named the child Ichabod, saying, The glory is departed from Israel: because the ark of God was taken, and because of her father in law and her husband.*

*And she said, The glory is departed from Israel: for the ark of God is taken.*

The word for "fail" in Habakkuk 3:17 means "to be untrue, in word (to lie, feign, disown) or deed (to disappoint, fail, cringe)." It is rendered in the King James Version as "deceive, deny, deal falsely, be found liars." Many Americans denied the Lord and deceived themselves in the 1992 presidential election. Since then, our chosen leaders have lied repeatedly, vacillating on important issues at the slightest political whim. None of us have anything to be proud of when journalists tag our Commander-in-Chief as "Slick Willie" or "President Pinocchio."

Amos 8:11-13, NIV:

*"The days are coming," declares the Sovereign Lord, "when I will send a famine through the land—not a famine of food or a thirst for water, but a famine of hearing the words of the Lord.*

*"Men will stagger from sea to sea and wander from north to east, searching for the word of the Lord, but they will not find it.*

*"In that day the lovely young women and strong young men will faint because of thirst."*

Habakkuk has not painted a very pretty picture. The famine for hearing the Word of God (the fig tree), and the woeful lack of the Holy Spirit (the olive tree) has emptied the field, the flock, and the fold. This nation was built upon the Bible. The Church was once relevant in America, ablaze by the Spirit. Now, all we sense is an eerie uneasiness.

Eccles. 10:1, KJV:

*Dead flies cause the ointment of the apothecary to send forth a stinking savour: so doth a little folly him that is in reputation for wisdom and honour.*

Eccles. 10:1, TLB:

*Dead flies will cause even a bottle of perfume to stink! Yes, a small mistake can outweigh much wisdom and honor.*

The lampstand in Moses' sanctuary and the torch in the lady's hand in New York harbor are smoldering. Why has the fire, the passion for God and country, gone out in men's hearts?

Satan is "beelzebub," "the lord of flies," the god of the dunghill (Lk. 11:15-19). The ointment is crowded with his willing servants, men and women who have traded their souls for temporal wealth and fame. There's a bad smell in Washington. God intended the office of the President, the ministry of the pastor in the local church, and the role of the father in the home to be reputed places of wisdom and honor. Without God's Spirit to guide them, men are making serious mistakes.

The prophet continues: The cultivated fields "yield" or "make" no "meat" or "food." Men labor for that which satisfies not (Is. 55:1-3). New policies are not working. Global economics are out of whack. Churches have fished all night, but caught nothing (Lk. 5:5). What worked yesterday is not working today.

The flock is "cut down" or "destroyed" from the "fold." This word in Habakkuk 3:17 means "a pen for flocks" and comes from a root meaning "to restrict, by act (hold back or in) or word (prohibit)." The Constitution of the United States established the legal principles that were intended to govern our nation. Radical leftists want no such guidelines. Especially since 1947 (separation of church and state), 1962 (prayer taken out of America's schools), and 1973 (*Roe v. Wade*), men have cut up our founding document like Jehoiakim shredded the original Book of Jeremiah.

The "fold" is also the local church (Ps. 78:70). Many Christians despise any kind of government or order. Parachurch ministries abound because no covenant commitment is required. No one wants any restrictions (Judg. 21:25). Folks just want to do their own thing in the name of the Lord, demanding covenant with Him on their own terms. If they do attend a local church, it is the church of their "choice," not where God has purposed to "set" them.

Ps. 68:6, KJV:

*God setteth the solitary in families: He bringeth out those which are bound with chains: but the rebellious dwell in a dry land.*

1 Cor. 12:18, KJV:

*But now hath God set the members every one of them in the body, as it hath pleased Him.*

The word for "herd" in Habakkuk 3:17 means "beef cattle; ox (as used for plowing)." The word for "stalls" means "a stall for cattle (from their resting place)." In the natural, the family farm is becoming a thing of the past in America. The work ethic is in shambles. In the spirit, no one is breaking any new ground. We hear the same old cabbage every Sunday morning and every Wednesday night. The work load of the average local church is carried by only 20 percent of its members. In the average Spirit-filled church in America, only 29 percent are consistent tithers. No one wants to shoulder any responsibility. No one wants to plow.

Is. 26:17-18, KJV:

*Like as a woman with child, that draweth near the time of her delivery, is in pain, and crieth out in her pangs; so have we been in Thy sight, O Lord.*

*We have been with child, we have been in pain, we have as it were brought forth wind; we have not wrought any deliverance in the earth; neither have the inhabitants of the world fallen.*

Eph. 4:14, NIV:

*Then we will no longer be infants, tossed back and forth by the waves, and blown here and there by every wind of teaching and by the cunning and craftiness of men in their deceitful scheming.*

All is barren. The Church has come to the time of birth (Rev. 12:1-5), but has only brought forth the wind of doctrine. "Escapist" theology and eschatology is no longer relevant (and has never been the issue). We have not brought any salvation or deliverance to America or the earth, nor can we until we see Habakkuk's vision. The creation is still sobbing. Worldly leaders and people haven't fallen; the devil and his crowd seem to be having their day.

God, where are You?

### Jesus Is Our Joy and Peace

The previous verse captures Habakkuk's beginning emotions and encapsulates the entire first chapter of his prophecy. Judah cannot exist without the fruit, the flocks, and the fold. America is cursed without the parallel of spiritual realities, the Judeo-Christian ethic of the founding fathers.

But the prophet's "burden" had taken him to the watchtower to receive the "vision" of the Lord. Transformed by God's own faith, Habakkuk's "prayer" breaks forth in song:

Hab. 3:18, KJV:

*Yet I will rejoice in the Lord, I will joy in the God of my salvation.*

Hab. 3:18, TLB:

*Yet I will rejoice in the Lord; I will be happy in the God of my salvation.*

Hab. 3:18, AMP:

*Yet I will rejoice in the Lord, I will exult in the (victorious) God of my salvation!*

The Hebrew word for "rejoice" here is *âlaz* (aw-laz) (Strong's #5937) and means "to jump for joy; to exult." It is rendered in the King James Version as "be joyful, rejoice, triumph." It is used 16 times in the Old Testament, including 7 times (complete rejoicing) in the Book of Psalms:

Ps. 28:7, KJV:

*The Lord is my strength and my shield; my heart trusted in Him, and I am helped: therefore my heart greatly rejoiceth; and with my song will I praise Him.*

Ps. 60:6, KJV:

*God hath spoken in His holiness; I will rejoice, I will divide Shechem, and mete out the valley of Succoth.*

Ps. 68:4, KJV:

*Sing unto God, sing praises to His name: extol Him that rideth upon the heavens by His name JAH, and rejoice before Him.*

Ps. 94:3, KJV:

*Lord, how long shall the wicked, how long shall the wicked triumph?*

Ps. 96:12, KJV:

*Let the field be joyful, and all that is therein: then shall all the trees of the wood rejoice.*

Ps. 108:7, KJV:

*God hath spoken in His holiness; I will rejoice, I will divide Shechem, and mete out the valley of Succoth.*

Ps. 149:5, KJV:

*Let the saints be joyful in glory: let them sing aloud upon their beds.*

The prophet Zephaniah knew about the Day of the Lord, the "day of trouble." He uses this same word for "rejoice" in his prophecy:

Zeph. 3:14, NIV:

*Sing, O Daughter of Zion; shout aloud, O Israel! Be glad and rejoice with all your heart, O Daughter of Jerusalem!*

Habakkuk 3:18 shows the powerful reality of resting in the Lord. The fruit of His peace is His joy and strength (Neh. 8:10). The word for "joy" here is stronger than the word for "rejoice." To "joy" is to "spin around under the influence of violent emotion"! It is used 18 times in the Book of Psalms and 11 times in the Book of Isaiah, as well as in these:

1 Chron. 16:31, KJV:

*Let the heavens be glad, and let the earth rejoice: and let men say among the nations, The Lord reigneth.*

Prov. 23:24, KJV:

*The father of the righteous shall greatly rejoice: and he that begetteth a wise child shall have joy of him.*

Song 1:4, KJV:

*Draw me, we will run after thee: the king hath brought me into his chambers: we will be glad and rejoice in thee, we will remember thy love more than wine: the upright love thee.*

Joel 2:23, KJV:

*Be glad then, ye children of Zion, and rejoice in the Lord your God: for He hath given you the former rain moderately, and He will cause to come down for you the rain, the former rain, and the latter rain in the first month.*

Zeph. 3:17, KJV:

*The Lord thy God in the midst of thee is mighty; He will save, He will rejoice over thee with joy; He will rest in His love, He will joy over thee with singing.*

Zech. 9:9, KJV:

*Rejoice greatly, O daughter of Zion; shout, O daughter of Jerusalem: behold, thy King cometh unto thee: He is just, and having salvation; lowly, and riding upon an ass, and upon a colt the foal of an ass.*

Zech. 10:7, KJV:

*And they of Ephraim shall be like a mighty man, and their heart shall rejoice as through wine: yea, their children shall see it, and be glad; their heart shall rejoice in the Lord.*

And all without drugs, alcohol, or illicit sex! The only true and lasting Source of real joy is the Lord. Happiness requires a "happening," and the next happening has to be bigger, better, badder, and wilder than the last. Happiness is temporal; joy is eternal. Joy is not based upon anything circumstantial. Joy is pure, uninhibited emotion, pouring from the heart of God Himself (Rom. 5:5).

Acts 2:15-18, KJV:

*For these are not drunken, as ye suppose, seeing it is but the third hour of the day.*

> *But this is that which was spoken by the prophet Joel;*
>
> *And it shall come to pass in the last days, saith God, I will pour out of My Spirit upon all flesh: and your sons and your daughters shall prophesy, and your young men shall see visions, and your old men shall dream dreams:*
>
> *And on My servants and on My handmaidens I will pour out in those days of My Spirit; and they shall prophesy.*

It's sad to see men and women, young and old, who have a problem with alcohol or drugs. Those habits are expensive and life-threatening. There's something better. Let's all go down to "Joel's Place" for a drink of "real" wine! And the best part is, it's free to "whosoever will"!

Is. 55:1, KJV:

> *Ho, every one that thirsteth, come ye to the waters, and he that hath no money; come ye, buy, and eat; yea, come, buy wine and milk without money and without price.*

Who or what is the source of all this joy? Habakkuk had (and I pray by this time you have) a vision of the "God of (his) salvation," a vision of "Jesus"! He had seen the One whose very name means "salvation, liberty, deliverance, and prosperity." This word is used 20 times in the Book of Psalms and 5 times in the Book of Isaiah, as well as in Habakkuk 3:13 to tell of our Savior.

Jesus is our Joy because Jesus is our Peace. Peace is the foundation of joy. Security begets expression.

Is. 55:12, KJV:

> *For ye shall go out with joy, and be led forth with peace: the mountains and the hills shall break forth*

*before you into singing, and all the trees of the field shall clap their hands.*

Rom. 14:17, KJV:

*For the kingdom of God is not meat and drink; but righteousness, and peace, and joy in the Holy Ghost.*

Rom. 15:13, KJV:

*Now the God of hope fill you with all joy and peace in believing, that ye may abound in hope, through the power of the Holy Ghost.*

Gal. 5:22, KJV:

*But the fruit of the Spirit is love, joy, peace, longsuffering, gentleness, goodness, faith.*

### The Rest That Is Given and the Rest That Is Found

He is our Peace who has broken down every wall. The Prince of Peace has become the King, the Administrator of Peace (Is. 9:6-7; Heb. 7:1-2). Peace is rest. Rest is peace.

Eph. 2:14-17, KJV:

*For He is our peace, who hath made both one, and hath broken down the middle wall of partition between us;*

*Having abolished in His flesh the enmity, even the law of commandments contained in ordinances; for to make in Himself of twain one new man, so making peace;*

*And that He might reconcile both unto God in one body by the cross, having slain the enmity thereby:*

*And came and preached peace to you which were afar off, and to them that were nigh.*

Eph. 2:14, TLB:

*For Christ Himself is our way of peace. He has made peace between us Jews and you Gentiles by making us all one family, breaking down the wall of contempt that used to separate us.*

The Greek word for "peace" is *ĕirēnē* (*Strong's* #1515) and means "peace; by implication, prosperity." It is used throughout the New Testament, including:

Jn. 14:27, KJV:

*Peace I leave with you, My peace I give unto you: not as the world giveth, give I unto you. Let not your heart be troubled, neither let it be afraid.*

Rom. 5:1, KJV:

*Therefore being justified by faith, we have peace with God through our Lord Jesus Christ.*

Eph. 4:3, KJV:

*Endeavouring to keep the unity of the Spirit in the bond of peace.*

Phil. 4:7, KJV:

*And the peace of God, which passeth all understanding, shall keep your hearts and minds through Christ Jesus.*

1 Thess. 5:23, KJV:

*And the very God of peace sanctify you wholly; and I pray God your whole spirit and soul and body be preserved blameless unto the coming of our Lord Jesus Christ.*

Heb. 12:14, KJV:

*Follow peace with all men, and holiness, without which no man shall see the Lord.*

Jas. 3:18, KJV:

*And the fruit of righteousness is sown in peace of them that make peace.*

Those of us who have learned to "rest in the day of trouble" know these verses well. We have come to understand that His rest is progressive, as well as once-and-for-all. There is a rest that is "given" and a rest that is "found."

Habakkuk had prophesied (2:1-4) that his vision was yet for an "appointed time," or for the "festival." There are three Feasts of the Lord: Passover, Pentecost, and Tabernacles (Deut. 16:16). The Church in America has come through two Feasts, and now stands on the threshold of the third. We have experienced Jesus Christ as our Savior, the Passover Lamb (Jn. 1:29; 1 Cor. 5:7-8), and as the One who baptizes with the Holy Ghost, as He did on the Day of Pentecost (Acts 1:5; 2:4). We are about to meet Him in the "third day," in the third dimension, as Lord and King (Hos. 6:1-3)!

Acts 17:30, NIV:

*In the past God overlooked such ignorance, but now He commands all people everywhere to repent.*

We are now living in a serious time, the "day of trouble." God will no longer deal with America and the Church in America as children or teenagers. We are the most blessed nation on the earth. He is dealing with us now as sons, commanding us to renew our minds. All things are out of Him, and through Him, and into Him (Rom. 11:36). We are going "through" Him now. The living Word is the Filter through whom we all must pass. He is the flaming Sword that turns "every way" (Gen. 3:24; Heb. 4:12). Every sin—individually, corporately, nationally—that we have not faced is being dealt with now by the "Chaldeans."

Put plainly, He is not going to allow us to carry our "mess" into His Kingdom. He invites us all:

Mt. 11:28-30, KJV:

*Come unto Me, all ye that labour and are heavy laden, and I will give you rest.*

*Take My yoke upon you, and learn of Me; for I am meek and lowly in heart: and ye shall find rest unto your souls.*

*For My yoke is easy, and My burden is light.*

In the Feast of Passover, the Outer Court of His purposes, there is a rest that is "given." Our sins are forgiven and washed away by the blood of Jesus, and we experience peace "with" God. In the Feast of Tabernacles, in the Most Holy Place, there is a rest that is "found." In the high calling of coming to the fullness of His stature, we experience the peace "of" God (Eph. 4:13; Heb. 6:19-20).

Sandwiched between Passover and Tabernacles is His "yoke" of covenantal discipline, the Feast of Pentecost.

The American Church has experienced childhood and adolescence in God, and is now being called to the place of maturity and full responsibility (Phil. 3:12-14).

Hos. 6:1-3, KJV:

*Come, and let us return unto the Lord: for He hath torn, and He will heal us; He hath smitten, and He will bind us up.*

*After two days will He revive us: in the third day He will raise us up, and we shall live in His sight.*

*Then shall we know, if we follow on to know the Lord: His going forth is prepared as the morning; and He shall come unto us as the rain, as the latter and former rain unto the earth.*

2 Pet. 3:8, KJV:

*But, beloved, be not ignorant of this one thing, that one day is with the Lord as a thousand years, and a thousand years as one day.*

Those who "rest in the day of trouble" will go on to know the Lord and be raised up in the third day. If you don't know Jesus as your personal Savior, come to Him now. He will give you rest. If you are a Christian, take His yoke upon you and learn of Him. He will bring you into the rest that is found, for the Feast of Tabernacles is a feast of "rest."

Ps. 94:12-13, KJV:

*Blessed is the man whom Thou chastenest, O Lord, and teachest him out of Thy law;*

*That Thou mayest give him rest from the days of adversity, until the pit be digged for the wicked.*

## The Feast of Tabernacles Is a Feast of Rest

Lev. 23:39, KJV:

*Also in the fifteenth day of the seventh month, when ye have gathered in the fruit of the land, ye shall keep a feast unto the Lord seven days: on the first day shall be a sabbath, and on the eighth day shall be a sabbath.*

All the Feasts of the Lord were observed in connection with sabbath days, but the Feast of Tabernacles is the real Feast of rest. It took place in the "seventh month," thus pointing to a time in God's purposes when the Church would come to completion, to maturity. Just as the weekly sabbath was the end of Israel's week of toil and labor, so the Feast of Tabernacles is the end of the Church's time of strife and turmoil.

Heb. 4:9, KJV:

*There remaineth therefore a rest to the people of God.*

This "rest" encompasses all that Habakkuk saw, for his "vision" beheld the finished work of Jesus Christ in His death, burial, resurrection, ascension, and coronation.

From Genesis to Revelation, God has ordained "rest" for the people of God, calling us to proceed from rest to rest, from glory to glory. Noah and the Flood, Ruth and Boaz, the Ark of the Covenant coming to Mount Zion as its final resting place—all these and more are pictures of our New Testament sabbath rest in Christ.

Num. 13:20, KJV:

*And what the land is, whether it be fat or lean, whether there be wood therein, or not. And be ye of good courage, and bring of the fruit of the land. Now the time was the time of the firstripe grapes.*

Like the 12 spies in the days of Moses, we have but tasted the firstfruits of the Spirit, the earnest of our inheritance (Rom. 8:23; Eph. 1:13-14). Let us be men of another spirit, like Caleb and Joshua, who believe that it is time to possess the whole land! It's time to bring America and the nations back to the Lord.

We have arrived at the last stanza of Habakkuk's prayerful song. The entire third chapter of his prophecy has been a marvelous panorama of Jesus' life and ministry. It is fitting that this final verse, like everything else, be unto Him!

# Chapter Ten

# The Person

## "To the Chief Singer"

### Habakkuk 3:19

Is. 9:6-7, KJV:

> *For unto us a child is born, unto us a son is given: and the government shall be upon His shoulder: and His name shall be called Wonderful, Counsellor, The mighty God, The everlasting Father, The Prince of Peace.*
>
> *Of the increase of His government and peace there shall be no end, upon the throne of David, and upon His kingdom, to order it, and to establish it with judgment and with justice from henceforth even for ever. The zeal of the Lord of hosts will perform this.*

Habakkuk's song is about to conclude, but the government and peace of the One it extols will never end!

After everything that can be shaken has been shaken (Heb. 12:25-29), all that remains is a King and a Kingdom that cannot be removed. Behold the King! Behold His *Person*! He is the Lord God, your strength!

Hab. 3:19, KJV:

*The Lord God is my strength, and He will make my feet like hinds' feet, and He will make me to walk upon mine high places. To the chief singer on my stringed instruments.*

Hab. 3:19, NIV:

*The Sovereign Lord is my strength; He makes my feet like the feet of a deer, He enables me to go on the heights. For the director of music. On my stringed instruments.*

Hab. 3:19, TLB:

*The Lord God is my strength; He will give me the speed of a deer and bring me safely over the mountains. (A note to the choir director: When singing this ode, the choir is to be accompanied by stringed instruments.)*

Hab. 3:19, AMP:

*The Lord God is my strength, my personal bravery and my invincible army; He makes my feet like hinds' feet, and will make me to walk [not to stand still in terror, but to walk] and make [spiritual] progress upon my high places [of trouble, suffering or responsibility]!*

Hab. 3:19, Ferrar Fenton:

*...To the Leader of My singers.*

Thine, O Lord Jesus, is the Kingdom, the power, and the glory. The song we are singing is unto You, out of You...it *is* You!

David, the sweet psalmist of Israel, sat in his tent and sang unto the Lord. When the Lord saved each of us, He said (as David declared to his son Solomon), "I've defeated all your enemies. Now take My provision and build your life, your home, your family, your ministry, your local church...your nation!"

Neh. 8:10, ASV:

*Then he said unto them, Go your way, eat the fat, and drink the sweet, and send portions unto him for whom nothing is prepared; for this day is holy unto our Lord: neither be ye grieved; for the joy of Jehovah is your strength.*

America, the Lord God is your "strength"! This Hebrew word in Habakkuk 3:19 means "a force, whether of men, means, or other resources; an army; wealth, virtue, valor, strength." It comes from a primitive root which means "to twist or whirl (in a circular or spiral manner); to dance." This is a powerful word, translated in the following verses as follows:

Deut. 8:18, KJV:

*But thou shalt remember the Lord thy God: for it is He that giveth thee power to get **wealth**, that He may establish His covenant which He sware unto thy fathers, as it is this day.*

Ruth 3:11, KJV:

*And now, my daughter, fear not; I will do to thee all that thou requirest: for all the city of my people doth know that thou art a **virtuous** woman.*

2 Sam. 22:33, KJV:

*God is my* **strength** *and power: and He maketh my way perfect.*

2 Sam. 22:40, KJV:

*For Thou hast girded me with* **strength** *to battle: them that rose up against me hast Thou subdued under me.*

Ps. 118:16, KJV:

*The right hand of the Lord is exalted: the right hand of the Lord doeth* ***valiantly.***

Is. 60:5, KJV:

*Then thou shalt see, and flow together, and thine heart shall fear, and be enlarged; because the abundance of the sea shall be converted unto thee, the* **forces** *of the Gentiles shall come unto thee.*

God is America's Source! Where do we find such strength? Away up on the mountaintop, on the watchtower of prayer and communion.

Once we are strengthened, He will "make" our feet like hinds' feet, and "make us" to walk. In his immaturity, the younger prodigal of Luke 15 said, "give me"; in repentance and humility, he later cried, "make me"! The name of Habakkuk's sob in chapter 1 was "give me"! The name of Habakkuk's song in chapter three is "make me!"

Ps. 37:23, KJV:

*The steps of a good man are ordered by the Lord: and He delighteth in his way.*

Ps. 119:133, KJV:

*Order my steps in Thy word: and let not any iniq-uity have dominion over me.*

2 Cor. 12:18, KJV:

*I desired Titus, and with him I sent a brother. Did Titus make a gain of you? walked we not in the same spirit? walked we not in the same steps?*

1 Pet. 2:21, KJV:

*For even hereunto were ye called: because Christ also suffered for us, leaving us an example, that ye should follow His steps.*

The word for "make" here in Habakkuk's last verse means "to put." God will "put" or "place" our feet. This entire song is about Jesus, the One who showed man where to walk and how to walk. If we get tired of walk-ing, we can always ride in His chariot (Hab. 3:13). He makes our "feet," literally our "steps," to be like that of the "hind," the female deer, known for the following:

1. *Agility and grace.*
2. *Ability to sense danger quickly.*
3. *Swiftness.*

There is a grace that is sufficient to walk through every trial and test. God will do this for America and the Church if we will but sing unto Him. Consider these verses about the "hind."

Gen. 49:21, KJV:

*Naphtali is a hind let loose: he giveth goodly words.*

Ps. 29:9, KJV:

*The voice of the Lord maketh the hinds to calve, and discovereth the forests: and in His temple doth every one speak of His glory.*

Song 2:7, KJV:

*I charge you, O ye daughters of Jerusalem, by the roes, and by the hinds of the field, that ye stir not up, nor awake my love, till he please.*

The word for "walk" in Habakkuk 3:15 and 19 is the same and means "to tread; by implication, to walk; also to string a bow (by treading on it in bending)." Consider again Habakkuk 3:9 and what was said about the "bow" and the covenant. To "tread" the bow is to walk in covenant with the Lord. This word is used in the following verses:

Josh. 1:3, KJV:

*Every place that the sole of your foot shall tread upon, that have I given unto you, as I said unto Moses.*

Ps. 91:13, KJV:

*Thou shalt tread upon the lion and adder: the young lion and the dragon shalt thou trample under feet.*

Amos 9:13, KJV:

*Behold, the days come, saith the Lord, that the plow-man shall overtake the reaper, and the treader of grapes him that soweth seed; and the mountains shall drop sweet wine, and all the hills shall melt.*

Zech. 9:13, KJV:

*When I have bent Judah for Me, filled the bow with Ephraim, and raised up thy sons, O Zion, against thy sons, O Greece, and made thee as the sword of a mighty man.*

And where are we to walk? In the "high" or "elevated" places. God enables us to go forth on the heights. He will bring us safely over every peak and precipice. Our Heavenly Bridegroom has invited us to the top of the mountain. We are called to walk and live in heavenly places (Eph. 1:3; 2:6).

Song 4:8, KJV:

*Come with me from Lebanon, my spouse, with me from Lebanon: look from the top of Amana, from the top of Shenir and Hermon, from the lions' dens, from the mountains of the leopards.*

The name of His mountain, His Kingdom and covenant, is "Amana" or "amen." This is the Hebrew word for "faith" and speaks of that which is "certain," sure, steadfast, immovable (2 Cor. 1:20). This way of life is in the heavenlies above the roaring of the lion and the den of the leopard, far above all principalities and powers. It is Job's undiscovered path and Isaiah's highway to Zion. It is the place of transcendent prayer, raising men above their present circumstances. Both Testaments describe this upward call and walk with the Lord.

Job 28:7-8, KJV:

*There is a path which no fowl knoweth, and which the vulture's eye hath not seen:*

*The lion's whelps have not trodden it, nor the fierce lion passed by it.*

Ps. 77:19-20, KJV:

*Thy way is in the sea, and Thy path in the great waters, and Thy footsteps are not known.*

*Thou leddest Thy people like a flock by the hand of Moses and Aaron.*

Is. 35:8-10, KJV:

*And an highway shall be there, and a way, and it shall be called The way of holiness; the unclean shall not pass over it; but it shall be for those: the wayfaring men, though fools, shall not err therein.*

*No lion shall be there, nor any ravenous beast shall go up thereon, it shall not be found there; but the redeemed shall walk there:*

*And the ransomed of the Lord shall return, and come to Zion with songs and everlasting joy upon their heads: they shall obtain joy and gladness, and sorrow and sighing shall flee away.*

Eph. 2:6, KJV:

*And hath raised us up together, and made us sit together in heavenly places in Christ Jesus.*

Phil. 3:20, KJV:

*For our conversation is in heaven; from whence also we look for the Saviour, the Lord Jesus Christ.*

Habakkuk has nothing else to say. All he can do now is behold the Lord! The prophet, himself a temple musician, sees Jesus as the "Chief Singer," or "Choir Director." Consider these parallels:

Eph. 2:20, KJV:

*And are built upon the foundation of the apostles and prophets, Jesus Christ Himself being the chief corner stone.*

1 Pet. 2:6, KJV:

*Wherefore also it is contained in the scripture, Behold, I lay in Sion a chief corner stone, elect, precious: and he that believeth on Him shall not be confounded.*

The New Testament word for "chief" in these two verses means "belonging to the extreme corner."

1 Pet. 5:4, KJV:

*And when the chief Shepherd shall appear, ye shall receive a crown of glory that fadeth not away.*

The Greek word used here is *archipŏimēn*, meaning the "head or ruling shepherd."

Jesus is the Chief Cornerstone and the Chief Shepherd. Jesus is the "Chief Singer." The similar phrase, "to the chief musician," is found in the inscriptions over exactly 50 (the number of Pentecost, Jubilee, anointing) of the Psalms (see 4–6; 8–9; 11–14; 18–22; 31, 36; 39–42; 44–49; 51–62; 64–70; 84–85; 88; 109; 139; and 140).

The New Testament, quoting the Psalmist, declares Jesus to be the Chief Singer, the Chief Musician.

Ps. 22:22, KJV:

> *I will declare Thy name unto my brethren: in the midst of the congregation will I praise Thee.*

Ps. 22:22, TLB:

> *I will praise You to all my brothers; I will stand up before the congregation and testify of the wonderful things You have done.*

The Hebrew word for "praise" here means "to be clear (of sound); to shine; hence, to make a show, to boast; and thus to be (clamorously) foolish; to rave; to celebrate." This is the Spirit of the Son in the midst of the Church (Gal. 4:6), always singing unto the Father. No one ever sobbed like the Lamb of God, and no one can sing like Jesus, the Chief Singer. Those who sob with Him will sing with Him (Rom. 8:17)!

Heb. 2:12, KJV:

> *Saying, I will declare Thy name unto My brethren, in the midst of the church will I sing praise unto Thee.*

Heb. 2:12, TLB:

> *For He says in the book of Psalms, "I will talk to My brothers about God My Father, and together we will sing His praises."*

The Greek word for "sing" here is *apalgéo* and means "to cease to feel pain for; to be past feeling." This powerfully describes the place of *complete rest* that our Lord has entered (Heb. 4:10).

While here in the flesh, Jesus lived and walked in the "high places," transcending the sense realm of feeling. He constantly sang to the Father (Jn. 8:29). He did feel pain. He carried our griefs and sorrows. But He declared, "It is finished!"—in that moment He ceased from His labors and entered into rest!

The Hebrew word for "chief singer" in Habakkuk 3:19 is *nâtsach* (Strong's #5329) and means "to glitter from afar, to be eminent (as a superintendent, especially of the Temple services and its music); to be permanent." *Vine's Dictionary* adds "keep, oversee, have charge over."

Jesus Christ is the Light of the world (Jn. 8:12); He shall always have the preeminence (Col. 1:18); He is the same yesterday, today, and forever (Heb. 13:8). He is the Shepherd and Overseer of our souls (1 Pet. 2:25). *Nâtsach* is used in First Chronicles 15:21; 23:4; Second Chronicles 2:2,18; 34:12-13; and Ezra 3:8-9 and is translated as "excel, set forward, oversee, overseers."

Finally, the word for "stringed instruments" here in verse 19 is the Hebrew *negîynâh*, which means "instrumental music; a stringed instrument; a poem set to music; an epigram." An epigram is a short, witty poem or saying.

*Negînâh* is used in the title of Psalm 61. Its root *nâgan* means "to thrum, beat a tune with the fingers; to play on a stringed instrument; to make music." It is used in these verses:

Ps. 77:6, KJV:

*I call to remembrance my song in the night: I commune with mine own heart: and my spirit made diligent search.*

Is. 38:20, KJV:

*The Lord was ready to save me: therefore we will sing my songs to the stringed instruments all the days of our life in the house of the Lord.*

Lam. 5:14, KJV:

*The elders have ceased from the gate, the young men from their musick.*

In America and in the Church, there is no government or order because we have stopped "making music." Praise releases the presence and government of God. The joy of the Lord is to be our strength. Each day can be lived in a major key or a minor key, our life style a happy song or a sad song. In Acts 16, Paul the apostle and Silas the prophet determined to "make music," though they (as Roman citizens) had a legal right to complain.

Acts 16:25-26, KJV:

*And at midnight Paul and Silas prayed, and sang praises unto God: and the prisoners heard them.*

*And suddenly there was a great earthquake, so that the foundations of the prison were shaken: and immediately all the doors were opened, and every one's bands were loosed.*

Verse 25 literally reads, "...and the prisoners were listening." We're all making music. What is your song and who are you playing it to?

Whatever song you're singing, you're not playing it by yourself. You've either made a covenant with death and hell, or you've been washed in the New Testament blood of the Lamb. Depending on which bow you've identified with, you're either "strung out" on the devil or the Lord.

The Church is a many-membered stringed instrument in the hand of the Chief Singer. He has turned our sob into a song, our mourning into dancing. Most importantly, we are walking, living, and singing *together*!

Habakkuk's prophetic vision is for the "festival." Come to the Feast and behold the Lamb...in Passover, Pentecost, and Tabernacles.

There is nothing you have faced, are facing, or will ever face that the Lord Jesus has not conquered in your behalf. "God came from Teman...." As a man full of the Holy Ghost, He has been tested in every point, yet without sin. He is our hope and peace. Hallelujah!

What is going to happen in America? What is going to happen in the nations? What is going to happen in the Church? How are you and your family going to deal with it all?

The secret of knowing the answers to these questions is to understand that this entire song about Jesus Christ, from His birth to His lordship over all things, is upon "Shigionoth."

# Chapter Eleven

# Epilogue

### "...upon Shigionoth"

Our new leader has no respect for the word of the prophets. Our court systems are corrupt: judges are dishonest, the law is perverted, favoring the criminal—there is no justice. Our economy is in shambles. The lower classes, not to mention the jobless and homeless, reel under its weight. Unfair and higher taxes have become mismanaged funds, wasted on useless projects and programs. At one time, we were a leader among the nations; now we are mocked and jeered. Homosexuality and lesbianism are spreading throughout our society like a loathsome disease; it's even in our churches. Our national sin is abortion, and has been for decades. Men have turned from the one true God to worship idols of wood and stone. Violence and murder fill the streets of our cities. Our future is bleak. We have no heroes. It's every man for himself. Hope is dying in the hearts of our people. What hurts the most is that God has apparently abandoned us.

This is America?

No, this is the nation of Judah over 2,500 years ago.

## A Chapter-by-Chapter Overview

This epilogue is a brief summary of our treatise. My greatest concern for the reader is that he understand the purpose of this writing. It is vital that you and your family receive the Word of the Lord as revealed in the Book of Habakkuk, the Old Testament book of faith. To help your review of all that has been said, we have condensed and highlighted chapters one through ten.

Chapter One, "The Day of Trouble, 600 B.C.," introduced the Book of Habakkuk. This historical background, taken from the Books of Kings and Chronicles, as well as the internal evidence of the Book of Habakkuk, furnished a powerful picture of the prophet's contemporary scene. We learned about Habakkuk—the man, the moment (his era), and the message (his word to Judah and America).

Chapter Two paralleled pre-exilic Judah with "The Day of Trouble, the 1990s," revealing America's current economic, moral, and spiritual dilemma. The major national sins of abortion and homosexuality were given the most attention, along with our root sin of idolatry. Drawn from a strong bibliography, the information given is meant to be a call to prayer. The Chaldeans of economy, immorality (especially AIDS), and violence have already invaded our homeland. God's answer for Habakkuk then is God's answer for America now.

Chapters Three and Four covered the first chapter of Habakkuk's prophecy, revealing the "burden" of "sobbing faith." Chapter Three introduced *the problem*. The natural and spiritual condition of Judah (and God's seeming indifference to it all) caused the prophet to cry out, "How long?" and "Why?"

Chapter Four brought God's reply to Habakkuk's prayer and *the perplexity*. Jehovah was about to raise up the Chaldeans as the rod of His anger. He would judge the sinful nation of Judah by means of a more sinful nation. Habakkuk's attempts to reason with the Lord proved futile, so he resorted to his watchtower of prayer.

Chapters Five and Six were taken from the second chapter of Habakkuk's prophecy and described his "vision" of "seeing faith." Chapter Five related *the prayer* of the prophet and underscored the revelation of God's faith. The vision is about a Person—the "it" of the Old Covenant becomes the "He" of the New. The vision is yet for "the festival"—Passover, Pentecost, and Tabernacles. All will be fulfilled in Jesus and His glorious Church. The knowledge of the glory of the Lord will cover the earth as the waters cover the sea.

Chapter Six detailed *the purging* as God judges and removes His enemies. The seven earmarks of the Chaldean personality, then and now, were discerned. This was followed by a fivefold judgment upon Babylon. After true justice is meted out, the Judge of the whole earth takes the bench. Rest is secured. The Lord is in His holy temple.

Chapters Seven through Ten examined the third and final chapter of Habakkuk's prophecy, pouring forth the "prayer" of "singing faith." Chapter Seven revealed *the provision*—the mystery of godliness. God came from Teman—God came from the Seed of the woman. Jesus was the Word made flesh. By the Spirit, Habakkuk saw His glorious birth over 600 years before it happened.

Chapter Eight lauded *the procession*, the life and ministry of Jesus Christ, from His incarnation to His coronation. He is declared to be the Word of God, the Will of God, and the Water of God. Jesus is the Light of the world, the unveiling of the New Covenant, and the Spirit of the Son. We are a covenant people, sealed with water baptism and the baptism with the Holy Ghost. The three "selahs" revealed three levels of Christian maturity: the new birth by the Spirit, the Pentecostal experience of having the covenant written on our hearts, and the complete defeat of satan in our lives and nation. Jesus is the Champion of the ages, having wounded the head of satan and triumphing over all the hosts of darkness. He wins...we win!

Chapter Nine keynoted *the peace* of God that enables us to "rest in the day of trouble." When there is no visible evidence of God anywhere, we will rejoice. Living in Him, we behold the earth through His eyes—the way God sees it all the time. We will joy in the God of our salvation.

Chapter Ten brought us full circle, revealing once and for all the focus of Habakkuk's vision, *the Person* of the Lord Jesus Christ. He is the Chief Cornerstone, the Chief Shepherd, and the Chief Singer. In union with Him, we live and walk in heavenly places. Of all that we have spoken, this is the sum—everything, all that we are, have, and do, is unto *Him*!

Hab. 3:19, KJV:

> *The Lord God is my strength, and He will make my feet like hinds' feet, and He will make me to walk upon*

*mine high places. To the chief singer on my stringed instruments.*

## To the Chief Singer

God wants to transform your life and circumstances, to change your sob into His song. Everything depends on your attitude, your perspective, your point of view. Once you see the Lord, once you understand that God became a man so we could face and overcome life's struggles, you will begin to sing. Once you see the earth and its inhabitants through His eyes, you will "rest in the day of trouble."

Jn. 10:10, KJV:

*The thief cometh not, but for to steal, and to kill, and to destroy: I am come that they might have life, and that they might have it more abundantly.*

Jn. 10:10, NIV:

*The thief comes only to steal and kill and destroy; I have come that they may have life, and have it to the full.*

The secret of the "abundant life" is that it is lived *unto the Lord.* This was Habakkuk's revelatory conclusion. Everything in life—your health, your family, your finances, your church, your ministry, your nation—must be laid at His feet. God is bringing America to its knees. All must be "to the Chief Singer"!

Jesus Christ is the Chief Musician. His is the Kingdom, the power, and the glory forever. Those who sing (Ps. 68:32) and "rest in the day of trouble" will:

1. *Perform unto the Lord (Mt. 5:33).*
2. *Give thanks unto the Lord (Lk. 2:38).*
3. *Turn unto the Lord (Acts 11:21).*
4. *Cleave unto the Lord (Acts 11:23).*
5. *Live and die unto the Lord (Rom. 14:8).*
6. *Be joined unto the Lord (1 Cor. 6:17).*
7. *Be acceptable unto the Lord (Eph. 5:10).*
8. *Submit unto the Lord (Eph. 5:22).*
9. *Be well pleasing unto the Lord (Col. 3:20).*
10. *Give glory, honor, and power unto the Lord (Rev. 19:1).*

All is *unto the Lord.* Consider these other New Testament verses which set forth our living "to the Lord."

2 Cor. 8:5, KJV:

*And this they did, not as we hoped, but first gave their own selves to the Lord, and unto us by the will of God.*

Eph. 5:19, KJV:

*Speaking to yourselves in psalms and hymns and spiritual songs, singing and making melody in your heart to the Lord.*

Eph. 6:7, KJV:

*With good will doing service, as to the Lord, and not to men.*

Col. 3:16, KJV:

*Let the word of Christ dwell in you richly in all wisdom; teaching and admonishing one another in psalms and hymns and spiritual songs, singing with grace in your hearts to the Lord.*

Col. 3:23, KJV:

*And whatsoever ye do, do it heartily, as to the Lord, and not unto men.*

A further examination of the phrases "unto Him" and "to Him" in the New Testament will reveal an abundance of truth. All is to the Chief Singer. All is "unto Him."

2 Cor. 5:15, KJV:

*And that He died for all, that they which live should not henceforth live unto themselves, but unto Him which died for them, and rose again.*

Eph. 3:21, KJV:

*Unto Him be glory in the church by Christ Jesus throughout all ages, world without end. Amen.*

2 Tim. 1:12, KJV:

*For the which cause I also suffer these things: nevertheless I am not ashamed: for I know whom I have believed, and am persuaded that He is able to keep that which I have committed unto Him against that day.*

1 Pet. 3:22, KJV:

*Who is gone into heaven, and is on the right hand of God; angels and authorities and powers being made subject unto Him.*

Rev. 5:13, KJV:

*And every creature which is in heaven, and on the earth, and under the earth, and such as are in the sea, and all that are in them, heard I saying, Blessing, and honour, and glory, and power, be unto Him that sitteth upon the throne, and unto the Lamb for ever and ever.*

All is unto the Chief Singer. All is "to Him."

Rom. 11:36, KJV:

*For of Him, and through Him, and to Him, are all things: to whom be glory for ever. Amen.*

1 Pet. 4:19, KJV:

*Wherefore let them that suffer according to the will of God commit the keeping of their souls to Him in well doing, as unto a faithful Creator.*

Rev. 1:6, KJV:

*And hath made us kings and priests unto God and His Father; to Him be glory and dominion for ever and ever. Amen.*

### Look Again!

Rev. 6:9-10, NIV:

*When He opened the fifth seal, I saw under the altar the souls of those who had been slain because of the word of God and the testimony they had maintained.*

*They called out in a loud voice, "How long, Sovereign Lord, holy and true, until You judge the inhabitants of the earth and avenge our blood?"*

Rev. 5:11-12, KJV:

*And I beheld, and I heard the voice of many angels round about the throne and the beasts and the elders: and the number of them was ten thousand times ten thousand, and thousands of thousands;*

*Saying with a loud voice, Worthy is the Lamb that was slain to receive power, and riches, and wisdom, and strength, and honour, and glory, and blessing.*

Are you sobbing or singing? Even in Heaven, there are two kinds of people—those who are still crying, "How long?" and those who are singing the worthiness of the Lamb.

I wrote this book for one reason: to bring hope to America and the Church in America. If you will hear these closing words with the same anointing with which they were penned, today will be a fresh beginning for you and all that concerns you.

Hab. 3:1, KJV:

*A prayer of Habakkuk the prophet upon Shigionoth.*

The word "Shigionoth" is mentioned only here in the entire Bible. In Habakkuk 3:1 it is given in the *plural* form. It is mentioned in the inscription over Psalm 7 (where David cried out to the Lord) in the singular form "Shiggaion."

"Shigionoth" (Strong's #7692) means "aberration; a dithyramb or rambling poem." It comes from the root word *shâgâh* (Strong's #7686) which means "to stray, mistake, or transgress; (through the idea of intoxication) to reel, be enraptured." It is translated as "ravished" (intoxicated with love) in Proverbs 5:19-20.

A "dithyramb" is a song with rapidly changing mood. Webster says that it is "any extravagantly emotional passage of prose or verse, wildly enthusiastic." This is music expressing strong, erratic emotion. Habakkuk's song was a hymn of great passion.

"Shigionoth" is in the same word family as *sha'ag*, which means "to cry aloud in trouble, danger, or pain."

"Shigionoth" means *to roar*...twice.

From the vantage of the watchtower, the place of transcendent prayer and worship, Habakkuk saw the Word made flesh over 600 years before it happened in a time-space world.

He looked the first time, and roared in *pain*.

The prophet saw Jesus in His *death*, dying on the cross for the sins of the world. His visage was marred more than any other. He was wounded for our transgressions and bruised for our iniquities. Habakkuk could hardly bear to behold sin that was exceeding sinful.

"Ah, Jehovah," he cried, "I cannot look again. The pain is too great. I beg of You, don't ever ask me to look at that again."

"You had to behold Me in My suffering, Habakkuk," Jehovah replied. "You will only have to see Me that way once, for My finished work was once-and-for-all. I have tasted death for every man. I have met the appointment. The penalty has been paid. It is finished."

"Now, My son, look again..."

Faith comes by hearing. Habakkuk obeyed the voice of the Lord and lifted his eyes once more.

He looked again, and roared in *praise*!

He now sees Jesus in His *resurrection*. The tomb is empty. The faithful High Priest has passed through the heavenlies and is the Word forever settled in Heaven. He is crowned with glory and honor. He is the legal covenantal Heir of all things in Heaven, in earth, and under the earth. He has been given all executive authority. His is the Name above every name. He is Lord!

Like our ancient prophetic friend, you and I must see the Lord. We must receive His Word and faith, and then look again...

All of us have sobbed. We have known the fellowship of His sufferings. We have learned how to be abased. Our spirits, souls, and bodies have known the pain of this world.

Your body may be in pain...

Your marriage hurting...

Your finances devastated...

Your children away from God...

Your local church splitting...

Your ministry seemingly over...

Your nation collapsing around you...

Your world falling apart...

In the name of the Lord Jesus Christ of Nazareth, I prophesy that you do LOOK AGAIN! There is fresh hope! Rest...in Jesus' name!

You have roared in *pain*...now you will roar in *praise*!

You have *sobbed*...now you will *sing*!

It's a new day for you and your family.

It's a new day for the Church.

It's a new day for America.

We see the bigger picture...bigger than Jehoiakim, Judah, and the Chaldeans. Bigger than Clinton, America, the economy, immorality, and violence.

Jesus is totally victorious. Nothing can hurt us now. We are at rest in the day of trouble...

"Shigionoth...." *Look again*!

## TAPE CATALOG

To receive a full listing of Pastor Varner's books and tapes, write or call for our current catalog:

Praise Tabernacle
P.O. Box 785
Richlands, NC 28574-0785
(910) 324-5026 or 324-5027

## TAPE OF THE MONTH

Each month two cassette tapes are made available by Pastor Varner. These messages are ministered by him and others in the five-fold ministry. You may join this growing list of listeners on a monthly offering basis.

## VIDEO CASSETTES

We are just beginning this new avenue of ministry. Presently available are three, two-hour video cassettes on the Book of Ruth. This teaching is a verse-by-verse exegesis concerning the Christian walk from conception to perfection, from birth to maturity. Please write or call for more information.

## SEMINARS AND CONVENTIONS

There are annual meetings here in Richlands for the Body of Christ. Please inquire for information on the next meeting. There is a team of ministry here at Praise Tabernacle that is available to your local church to teach the principles of restoration and assist in the areas of praise and worship. Please contact Pastor Varner.